THE CHARACTERS ON MY COUCH

A COLLECTION OF THERAPY SESSIONS WITH YOUR FAVORITE FILM AND TV CHARACTERS

PHIL STARK

TABLE OF CONTENTS

INTRODUCTION

I'm a therapist. My clients include people who come to me for support and guidance regarding experiences like relationship conflict, career struggles, parenting challenges, and divorce, among others. These experiences often cause feelings that are unpleasant to feel, including depression, anxiety, anger, and sadness, among others.

I enjoy my work. I find it inspiring and rewarding. However, for many years before becoming a therapist, I was a screenwriter. I made my living developing, pitching, and writing movies and TV shows. Often the most important aspect of the scripts I wrote, the thing about my projects that people got the most excited about, was the characters.

When I started out as a screenwriter, my characters were simple and underdeveloped. I would come up with an idea for a story, then create the characters that fit into the story, then direct these characters to do the things I needed them to do in order to advance the story. Later on in my career I became more curious about what the characters might want to do instead of what I wanted them to do. I began to write longer and more detailed biographies of these characters as preparation for writing scripts, and as I did this, the information I discovered about them began to inform the stories I wanted to tell.

I had always approached writing a screenplay like building a house, developing a detailed blueprint before ever picking up a hammer. However, the more time I spent exploring what these characters were like outside of the screenplay, the more often I realized that maybe they didn't want to do the things I needed them to do in order to tell the story I wanted to tell.

This was a big shift for me as a writer. Planning things out before writing a screenplay is safe. There is comfort in knowing what's going to happen before you write it. I found (and still find) it scary to think about starting to write without having everything figured out beforehand, to explore a story through the lens of the character and allow the discovery of who that character really is to inform the plot.

I remember reading interviews with screenwriters who talked about how they would sit down at their computer and let their characters tell them what they wanted to do. I thought that was crazy. Over time, however, I started to appreciate this approach. I spent more time figuring out what the characters wanted to do than what I wanted them do to. And I think this helped me create more realistic, compelling, and engaging characters.

Now that I'm a therapist, I work with the most realistic, compelling, and engaging characters of all: real people. Real people have all the complexity, internal conflict, and contradictions that the characters we see onscreen often lack. And no matter how much work a writer puts into creating these kinds of characters, if they don't understand what makes themselves tick as the main characters in the movie of their own lives, if they don't see how what they do and say today is informed by their past experiences and relationships, they will find it hard to create characters that are anywhere near as engaging and compelling as real people.

The clients in my practice are the main characters in the movies of their lives, and they come to me for help processing the powerful emotions from past experiences that affect their relationships in the present. Once we develop a greater awareness of the hidden emotional current guiding us down the river of life, we can recognize in specific moments how our own emotional material might prevent us from being happy in our relationships, or from achieving what we want in our careers, and begin to empower ourselves to steer our boat in a different direction.

In therapy we seek this car-tharsis, this process of releasing, and thereby providing relief from, strong or repressed emotions. We aspire to create change that mitigates the drama and conflict in our lives, leading us to a happier, more peaceful existence. The screenwriter's goal, however, is different. The screenwriter strives to create characters who act in ways that are at odds with their goals, or sabotage their relationships, or prevent themselves from achieving the things we root for them to achieve, and it is through this struggle that we identify or sympathize with them and become invested in their journey. I know that what engages me as a viewer are characters like this, and especially characters who struggle with these issues without understanding that they themselves are the source of their struggles.

The challenge here is that in order to empower themselves to change these things, a character must be aware of them. And if a character becomes aware of them and changes them, they will lead happier, more peaceful lives. And characters who are happier and more at peace with their lives experience less drama and conflict, which means as a viewer we might not find their stories as compelling or interesting as we do when their lives are full of drama and conflict. We don't want these characters to achieve the clarity and awareness that come with therapy, because we are entertained by their struggles. However we, as real people in real life, should welcome this clarity and awareness. Let us be entertained by fictional characters with fictional struggles and problems. Let our real lives be boring in their contentment!

This led me to consider characters from my favorite movies and TV shows, the inner conflicts and issues they struggle with, and why I find myself drawn to them. Why I find myself rooting for them to overcome the obstacles they encounter and achieve the goals they have for themselves. And being a therapist, I looked at them through the lens of therapy. What would happen if these characters were clients of mine? If Don Draper was in therapy, would it improve his relationships with women? Would Michael Corleone feel better after admitting to feelings of guilt about ordering the murder of his brother? Would couples therapy help Harry and Sally navigate their relationship after the movie ended?

This book is the answer to those questions, and others. It's an entertaining look at the inner lives of characters we have come to love (or hate). But no matter how much we admire, care about, or are intrigued by these characters, we are always aware that they are not real people. They were created by real people, however, and the real people who created these characters are the true artists. These writers and creators drew from their own personal experiences and those of others to fashion the fictional characters whose stories we are drawn to. They are flawed, they are conflicted, they struggle, they strive, and this is what keeps us coming back every week to see what happens next.

I hope you enjoy the exploration of these characters in a therapy setting, and if the material here intrigues you, let me encourage you to think about engaging in therapy yourself. You are the main character in the movie of your life, and if you find yourself struggling with experiences like relationship conflict, career struggles, parenting challenges, or divorce, among others, and these experiences are causing feelings that are unpleasant to feel, including depression, anxiety, anger, or sadness, among others, therapy can help. There's a section at the end of this book with resources to help you find a therapist. But don't skip ahead just yet. First enjoy reading about the therapy experiences of your favorite film and TV characters. Then you can have your own!

1

DON DRAPER

Intake Information: Client is a 42 year old male mandated to attend therapy following a forced leave of absence from executive position at an advertising agency. Client reports use of alcohol was a factor in this decision. Client is divorced and remarried, with three children from first marriage, and reports no previous therapy experience.

Don Draper sits on the couch across from me, wearing a suit and tie, shoes shined, hair slick, holding a fedora on his lap.

"So that's all there is to it? We just talk?" Don sounds skeptical.

"Pretty much," I reply. "I know it sounds simple, but it's what we talk about that can get complicated."

"Sounds about right." He sighs with resignation, then fishes a pack of cigarettes out of a pocket. "Well, let's get it over with."

He's about to light a cigarette when I speak up. "Sorry, but there's no smoking in here," I say, trying to sound sympathetic.

"Okay," Don says, surprised, as he puts away the cigarettes.

"In your intake paperwork, you indicated that your employer has mandated that you must attend therapy as a condition for keeping your job. Is that accurate?"

"Somewhat. This is a condition for me to keep my ownership stake in the agency. It's an advertising agency, and I'm a partner. A cofounder, to be more specific. But yes, your point is taken, which is that I'm not here voluntarily. And I'm sure you hear this a lot, but I don't really see why I need to be here at all."

"Well, according to your fellow partners, there are concerns about your (I read from my notes) 'heavy drinking and dark moods.'"

"Heavy drinking, my ass," Don scoffs. "One man's heavy drinking is another man's breakfast. And it's not like I'm the only one with a bar cart in his office. My colleague Roger's main source of hydration are the few times he puts ice in his vodka."

"So, the use of alcohol is tolerated in the office?"

"It's expected. And yes, I've seen plenty of colleagues be unable to handle their liquor, and have it affect their job performance negatively, but that's not me. I've always been able to handle my liquor."

"Until now?"

Don glares back at me. "Right. Until now."

"Would you say that your drinking has become a problem?"

"A problem? I wouldn't use that word."

"I can appreciate that. There are plenty of words we can use to describe things. Let me ask you a few questions that might help us assess your alcohol use. How many drinks do you have in a typical day?"

"Well let's see..." Don thinks to himself for a moment, counting in his head. "Four? Five? Unless I have a business dinner. Or lunch."

I nod, writing this down in my notes. "Do you ever drink more than you originally intend to?"

"That seems to be the pattern."

"Do you spend a significant amount of time recovering from your drinking?"

"I have been known to fall asleep on my couch every now and then."

"Have you ever tried to cut back on your drinking but found yourself unable to?"

"Okay, so it's a problem," says Don, exasperated. "But it's not just my problem. Everyone I know drinks. It comes with the territory. It's what kicks off every business meeting, every work dinner, it's the first martini with lunch, all the way to the last call with an important client at the end of the night."

"It sounds like there's a big drinking culture in your workplace."

"Absolutely. You're expected to drink. It's a given. And the guys who give up booze and go dry, they're looked down on. They don't get invited to the dinners where relationships are formed, where the real deals are consummated. Drinking and work go hand in hand."

"I see. So, alcohol had already been a part of your life, but recently it's gotten to be perhaps too big a part," I say. "And it sounds like there's some irony in the fact that your drinking goes hand in hand with your work, and you've been able to perform at a high level in the past while drinking, but that your current level of alcohol use has negatively affected your job performance."

"Yes, quite the irony."

Don fishes out a cigarette again, flicks open his Zippo and is about to light it, then catches my eye and realizes what he's doing.

"Sorry. Should we discuss my smoking habit?"

"Maybe in a future session. So, how exactly did the drinking negatively affect your job performance?"

Don thinks about this. "It didn't really. It made me feel looser creatively, more adept at pivoting during a pitch. It was a way to bond with clients. It certainly took the edge off the stresses of work. And home."

"Okay, but the negatives?"

Don thinks about this for a long moment.

"It made me tell the truth."

"About what?"

"About myself."

"What is the truth?"

Don shifts uncomfortably in his seat.

"What is the truth? Well Doc, I didn't have the greatest childhood. Long story short, I grew up in a whorehouse, and pretty early on I realized I wanted out. So I spent the early years of my life creating my own story. A new, better story. I pulled a real Horatio Alger, pulling myself up by my bootstraps, and now I live in the Big Apple, working with million dollar corporations and getting paid handsomely to sell their products to the teeming masses."

"That sounds pretty good," I observe.

"It does. And it is. But recently there was a meeting at work where I... I shared some details of my childhood that... Let's just say they didn't land well."

"Tell me a little more about your childhood."

Don doesn't respond right away. He sits with the thoughts that this question brings up. It feels like a sensitive subject.

After a long moment Don shrugs. "There's not much to tell. It wasn't great."

I wait silently for him to continue, but Don looks at me expectantly.

"If you're waiting for me to go into more detail about my traumatic childhood I hate to disappoint you, but I'd rather not."

"Okay, I get that. Of course, it's been my experience that in therapy, it's often the things we'd rather not discuss that are the most important things to discuss."

"Very wise of you, but I'm going to pass. In fact, I never thought I'd say this, but let's try and focus on my drinking."

"Okay. So, based on your experience at work, and what you've described regarding your history of alcohol use, the drinking has become a problem."

"I don't know, who's to say? I mean, I'll take a few weeks off, sober up, get to bed earlier, drink more milk, and eventually go back to work and carry on from there."

"And the drinking?"

"I suspect the drinking will continue. Only under control."

"Meaning, it's now out of control?"

"Well, I'm sitting here talking to you, aren't I?"

"Don, do you want to quit drinking?"

Don stops and thinks for a long moment.

"Do you want the truth? Or do you want what you think I think I want you to write down on that note pad?"

"I'll take the truth."

Don sighs. "I don't want to quit drinking. I just want to get back to work. It defines me. Without it, I'm scared of what I'll be. Or not be."

"Which, the drinking or work?"

Don considers this for a moment, then: "Both."

"Do you think when you eventually do go back to work, you'll be able to perform at the level your partners expect you to?" I ask.

"I do. This time off has actually been good for me. I've been able to focus on myself. Spend more time with my wife. See my kids more. It's amazing how much easier it is to cut back on drinking when you don't have people coming into your office every half hour asking if you want a drink."

Don takes a cigarette out of the pack and looks at it.

"I'm just going to hold this, if you don't mind."

"Have you been smoking long?"

Don laughs. "As long as I can remember. I smoke more than I drink. But smoking's the least of my problems."

"And what exactly are your problems?"

Don seems annoyed. "You and your probing questions."

I shrug. "Just doing my job."

He sits back and thinks. "What are my problems, let's see. The ad agency I started is threatening to kick me out. My kids hate me. Well, just my daughter, really. And my wife is great, but..."

Don clams up, and I sit in silence as this unfinished sentence hangs in the air, until he feels the need to change the subject.

"Look, I've been drinking just as much as I did when I first started in this business and nobody complained about it then. It's just what you do. It's just the way it is."

We sit in silence for another long moment. This time I break it.

"You said a moment ago that your wife is great, but..."

I wait for him to finish the sentence, but he doesn't.

"But what?" Don asks.

"That's what I'm curious about. The what."

He thinks for a long moment, confronting something he'd rather not confront.

"I do things that undermine our relationship."

"Is this related to your drinking?"

"Not exactly. But it certainly doesn't help. An idea that seems like a remote possibility sober can seem like a grand slam after three fingers of the brown stuff."

"Can you tell me about some of these ideas?"

Don sits for a long moment, thinking deeply.

"I've been unfaithful. Multiple times. With multiple women. In fact, I can't remember ever having a relationship where I was faithful. I don't know why. It just seems to happen."

Don stares off into the distance wistfully as he continues. "I was unfaithful in my marriage. My first one. And my second one. The current one, I mean. I just find myself attracted to other women. I crave their attention. And it doesn't matter how attractive my wife is. I mean, Megan is a television actress, for Pete's sake. She's gorgeous. She's the kind of woman men fall over each other for just to light her cigarette. And yet I find myself seeking out others."

Don sits with what he's just said, holding the unlit cigarette, examining it but thinking about something else.

"I have a dark history, Doc. My childhood, growing up, the war..."

"Which war?"

"I was in Korea. But I don't want to get into it, that's a whole other ball of wax."

"Might any of that be related to your drinking?"

"Most likely, but like I said, I don't want to get into that."

"I can appreciate that, but it's often the case—"

"I know, whatever I say I don't want to get into is obviously what I should be getting into. But remember, I'm not here voluntarily, this is a work requirement, and I just want to do the minimum of whatever I have to do here with you in order to get back to work."

"Fair enough."

A long silence. This time I break it. "What drew you to work in advertising?"

"I've always been good at selling things. At first it was cars, fur coats, whatever needed selling. But with advertising, I'm not really selling things. I'm selling ideas. Of course, selling ideas leads to people buying things. And I'm good at it. I'm really good at it."

"What makes you so good at it?" I ask.

Don cocks his head as he thinks about how to explain this.

"I understand what people want. Not what brand of cigarettes they prefer, or which fast food restaurant has the best burger, or which airline has the prettiest stewardesses. It's something more mysterious than that. It's about the longing we each have deep inside us, that thing we feel is lacking in our lives. We each have a hole in ourselves that we spend our lives trying to fill. And I sell shovels."

"That's interesting. What if you had to create an ad for yourself?"

"What do you mean?"

"I mean, if there was an ad that described the current state of your life, what would it look like?"

Don chuckles softly.

"It's funny that you ask that. It's basically what got me fired. Or, suspended, I should say. I was pitching an ad for Hershey's. Wholesome, family, love, safety. It's my job to evoke these feelings in a consumer and then have them associate those feelings with the product. But what I pitched was too sad. Too revealing. I shared a memory that was very real, but not exactly wholesome. And I knew while I was doing it it was wrong, but... I felt compelled to do it."

Don sniffles, having gotten emotional during this speech. I slide the box of Kleenex on the table towards him, but he takes out his own handkerchief and dabs at a nascent tear.

"You know, you were referred to me to discuss your drinking, and we discussed that, and then moved into a discussion of your marital struggles, your infidelity, but it strikes me that whatever you're feeling right now might be the true source of the issues that led you here."

"I was afraid you were going to say something like that." With that, Don composes himself and stands up. "Are we done here?"

"Actually, no, we have a few minutes left."

"Well, sorry to cut things short, but I've got to catch the train back to the city. Do I have to come back?"

"Professionally speaking, I think there's more emotional material here that would be worth examining. But in relation to your therapy mandate, I think that would be a more appropriate question for your partners. Or your lawyer."

"Great thanks. I'll have my girl call yours."

Don grabs his hat and overcoat as I cross over to open the door for him. I hear his Zippo flick and spark as he lights a cigarette on his way out.

I close the door behind him, then sit down to write up my notes.

Clinical Notes: Client presented with a confident affect, discussing his relationship with alcohol and the pervasiveness of alcohol use in the advertising industry. Client is mandated to attend therapy by terms of agreement with partners at advertising agency, which he was suspended from as a result of behavior resulting from alcohol use. Client discussed his drinking habits, how they fit into his work experience, a childhood he described as being traumatic, his marital struggles (divorce, infidelity), and towards end of session, revealed that the reason for his suspension was linked to revelations about his traumatic childhood in front of agency clients, which Client declined to go into detail about. Client left session early, and Therapist is unsure whether treatment will continue.

Diagnosis:

F10.20: Alcohol Use Disorder, Moderate

Z63.0: Relationship Distress with Spouse or Partner

2

KENDALL ROY

Intake information: Client is a 39 year old man seeking therapy for support in relationship with his father. Client reports working in the family business, and experiencing conflict with father related to business dealings and succession planning, which is rooted in deep-seated relationship dynamics. Client also reports conflict with siblings in regards to similar issues, as well as the use and possible abuse of drugs and alcohol. Client is divorced, with two children, and Client reports some previous therapy experience with family therapy.

I'm sitting in my chair, ten minutes past the hour, wondering if my new client is going to show up, when suddenly the office door opens and Kendall Roy enters, wearing an expensive suit and sunglasses, which he removes and hands to a young woman trailing him, carrying two work bags and several phones.

Kendall is in mid-conversion. "Get Stewy oiled up, hint to Naomi that there'll be a reach-out slash reach-around in the near-term short-term, and lock up Ichabod Crane before he pees his pants."

The woman types quickly on one of the phones. "Got it. And Ichabod Crane is..."

"Greg the Egg. Come on Jess, I pay you to keep up with the nicknames."

Kendall stops and acknowledges me. "You must be Phil."

"That's me," I say. We shake hands, then Kendall checks his watch.

"I'm New York late, but LA on time," he says as he sits down on the couch across from me. "So, let's do this! Let's tie up my superego and beat it into submission, yeah?"

I'm about to respond when Jess breaks in, reading off one of the phones. "They're saying 2pm Eastern, so we'll have a one hour exclusive window with favored nations to shape the narrative before we go wide."

"Love it. And I honestly don't care which jet it is, but make sure it's the big one. Now go sit in the corner while I get mind fucked."

Kendall turns back to me. "Sorry, here I am walking into your office and already fucking shit up. But I'm here, ready to dive into the depths of my inner self."

"I'm glad to see your enthusiasm, but traditionally the only people in the room during therapy are the therapist and the client," I say, referring to Jess.

"Oh, don't worry about her, she signed an iron-clad NDA. I actually own naming rights to her first born."

Jess looks up from her phone. "What?"

"I'm afraid this is a sticking point for me," I admit.

Kendall looks confused. "Okay, but, certainly you can make an exception here? I mean, I'm juggling billion dollar balls in an orgy of multi-tasking. I'll double your fee. Triple it. Come on, what's your number?"

I think for a moment, then: "Ten million dollars worth of deep in the money call options in Waystar Royco."

Kendall thinks for a moment before erupting in laughter. Then he turns to Jess. "You heard the man, get the fuck out."

Jess gathers her things, and reminds Kendall as she crosses out: "Just keep in mind we have a hard out, the chopper's holding, and if we don't—"

"Save it for future me, Jess," says Kendall, waving her away.

Jess exits. I sit for a moment, appreciating the silence. Kendall pats his legs with nervous energy. "That's better," he says. "Always nice to have few minutes to focus completely on myself. Mental health is so very important nowadays. So. What do we do?"

"I saw in your intake paperwork that you have some previous therapy experience?" I ask.

"Yeah, but that was just a PR stunt with my dad and the sibs, trying to calm the market, we didn't really get any emotional legwork done. That's why I reached out to you. '*Dude, Where's My Car-tharsis*?' That's right, I read your book. Well, I had Jess read it. She thought it was cute."

I return the focus to Kendall. "And the primary reason for seeking therapy is your relationship with your father?"

"That's right. Things are complicated between us in the immediate timeline, and there's an even more complicated backstory. Like with most fathers and sons, especially ones whose companies have a forty percent share of the cable media market."

Kendall becomes more serious as he talks about this topic. "There's a classic love / hate thing happening here. I'm the first born son, I'm supposed to take over the family business, which is something the old man has always led me to believe would happen, but now I'm starting to think he's been cock-teasing me this whole time, and he'll never anoint me. Not while he's alive, at least. And he'll probably find a way to fuck me over from the grave."

I take all this in, trying to decide where to explore. "Has your relationship always been so antagonistic?"

"It feels like it. I mean, he was always prepping me to be his successor, so there was a feeling of acceptance. But the older I get, the more I think he sees me as his enemy. We're clearly in Oedipus territory here. Which is actually a great story, Oedipus, I'm looking into optioning the rights. It might just be the case that I have to kill my father to give birth to my fully realized self. In the metaphorical sense, of course. And don't worry, I have no desire to fuck my mom. Maybe a handjob. That's not incest right?"

I ignore the shock value and continue. "Our relationships with our fathers can certainly be challenging. Especially for you, when you work together in the way you do. Is there any separation between the business relationship and the personal?"

"None. He is the company, and the company is him, and if you come between him and what he wants, it doesn't matter if you're a cousin or the president, you're getting fucked."

I nod at this, writing it down in my notes, and then decide to pivot to another subject. "And, you said you have siblings?"

"Yes, two and a half. And believe me, this is the topic of every slumber party."

"Are their relationships with your father similarly complicated?"

"Yes, but I'm the chosen one, the eldest son. Our relationship is special. My father is larger than life. He's more than a person. He's an entity, a force. And growing up you learn to stay out of the way of that force, but as an adult, I find myself more often than not directly in the path of it. I thought I could ride the wave, but now it's clear it's crashing down on me."

"That sounds like a natural progression," I observe. "Our relationships with our parents and the conflict that can be involved is often something we avoid early on in life, but it can come to a head later on."

"That's exactly where we are now, at a head. He thinks I don't have what it takes to be in charge. He doesn't care about emotions or feelings. He only respects strength. Aggression. He thinks I'm not a killer."

Kendall sits for a moment, thinking, and I sit in the silence, waiting to see what comes up for him.

"Something happened," Kendall says, now serious. "An incident, an accident, in the past. Something I did. That was bad. So I went to my dad for help. And he helped me. He did what a dad's supposed to do. But now he's holding it against me. I mean, you're supposed to go to your dad for help with life's difficulties, right? And they're supposed to help you because they love you, not because it puts them in a strategically advantageous position. But, that's my dad. Every problem is an opportunity."

Kendall leans back again, still deep in thought. I pass on asking a question to let him continue to feel whatever he's feeling in the moment. After a moment he continues.

"He wants me to take the fall."

"For what?"

"The whole cruise ship department scandal. You heard about that, right?"

Before I can respond Kendall continues. "He wants me to be the fall guy. We had a big meeting, all the top brass, and it was determined that someone would have to take the bullet. Someone would have to be sacrificed. And it was decided that it should be me. I thought he would love me more if I did this. Like, by going along with this plan I would be proving myself to him. He'd finally be impressed with me. But I don't know if that will ever be the case."

"I can understand that," I say. "It's true, based on my experience working with similar parent relationships with other clients, that it's one thing to do the work to develop an understanding about what you needed from your parents and how they didn't provide it for you. To learn to verbalize exactly what you wish they would say to you that would make you feel better. The harder part is accepting the fact that they'll probably never say those things. They're just not capable of it. They might not ever be able to give you what you need."

Kendall nods as he considers this. "That's very true. I can't keep waiting for him, hoping that some day I'll do something that will earn his approval. I have to kill him."

I sit for a moment, waiting for him to elaborate, then I clarify: "Not literally though, right?"

"No. I mean, probably not. I mean, like five percent chance, max. But don't worry, my lawyers looked at your intake paperwork, you've got no liability. But if I want the crown, I gotta come for the king, and I best not miss."

Kendall looks up at me in a new, more determined manner.

"My father is a malignant presence. He's a bully, and a liar. I think it's time for his reign to end, and I'm the one to end it."

"That sounds like it's something you've thought about, with determination and clarity."

"Thanks, but I actually just came up with it in this moment."

Kendall snaps out of his contemplative mood and back to his more jocular self as he stands up.

"Hells yeah! Determination and clarity FTW. What a great session, right? This has been great. I'm really knocking this mental health ball out of the park, don't you think?"

"I'm glad you feel that way. Of course, we still have plenty of time left."

The thumping sound of a helicopter appears in the distance, becoming louder and louder.

Kendall ignores the sound and continues. "Does it always work like this with your clients? You should be scaling this operation, big time. Move past the individual client and apply this to multiples. You know, podcasts, AI, one flywheel spinning off into alternate revenue streams."

The helicopter sound is so loud now that Kendall has to raise his voice.

"I'll have my nerds put together a spreadsheet!"

Before I can respond the office door opens, and Jess appears, wearing a set of noise-cancelling headphones, and hands another pair to Kendall.

"We're ninety seconds off schedule!" Jess yells.

"I'm all done here, let's go!" yells Kendall, as he puts on the headphones.

"Kendall, are we on for next week?" I yell.

Kendall points to his headphones, indicating that he can't hear me, then offers me a fist bump before striding out of my office, Jess close on his heels.

I look out the window at the helicopter that's just landed in the parking lot. Kendall and Jess get on board and it flies away.

I sit back down in my chair and start to write up my notes.

Clinical Notes: Client presented with an upbeat affect, displaying a big personality, eager to joke and make light of serious issues. As session continued, Client became more introspective, considering his relationship with his father both in terms of his upbringing, and also present day business decisions. Client described frustration with wanting to take over the family business, and being told by father that was the plan, but confronting the reality that father might not really want to commit to a succession plan. Client ended session determined to take action to confront his father.

Diagnosis:

Z62.820: Parent-Biological Child Conflict

Z56.9: Unspecified Problem Related to Employment

3

CERSEI LANNISTER

Intake Information: Client is a 40 year old female mandated to attend therapy as the result of a court order. Requirement for therapy has to do with recent events involving work and family life, and what Client describes as "alleged crimes," as numerated by an authority referred to as the High Sparrow. Client reports feelings of anxiety and frustration, as well as lack of appetite. Client is a widow, has three children, and reports no previous therapy experience.

Cersei Lannister sits on the couch across from me, wearing a formless dirty brown dress, her hair shorn and sticking out at jagged angles. Her affect and posture are regal even as her clothes indicate otherwise. She looks around my office with a hint of disdain.

"This couch is uncomfortable. I'm not used to such formless furniture. I need something with more support. Do you have any chairs?"

"I'm sorry, I don't," I say. "I probably should have a chair, though, for clients who prefer one. I'll make note of that for the future. So tell me, Cersei. Why are you here?"

She smirks. "Doesn't it say why in those important looking papers of yours?"

I pick up her intake paperwork.

"It says here you're mandated to attend therapy as a 'requirement for your rehabilitation' as ruled by the High Sparrow. Who's that?"

Cersei scoffs. "Who is the High Sparrow? He's a worm, a tiny little man hiding behind the shield of religion. He's jealous of those with royal blood, and he wishes me ill."

"So is he, like, a judge?"

"Yes, as well as jury and executioner."

"And what is this rehabilitation he mentions?" I ask.

"I am to serve penance for my sins."

"What are these sins?"

"Do you exist simply to ask questions?" she says, annoyed.

"That's pretty much my job."

"And if I refuse to answer them?"

"Then you refuse."

"But I must remain here for the allotted time?"

"Fifty minutes. By ruling of the High Sparrow," I remind her. "But I can't force you to talk."

Cersei smiles wistfully. "I miss forcing people to talk. It can be quite satisfying."

She sighs, and sits back, seemingly happy to sit in silence, and I join her, waiting.

After a minute or so she appears restless, and leans back in. "What are my sins, you ask? What are anyone's sins? They are simply actions one takes that are judged by others differently than how one judges them one's self."

"So, sins are subjective."

"They are in this case. As a queen, I would say my sins should not even be considered sins by my subjects. Although I suppose technically I'm no longer a queen. And that's besides the point for the High Sparrow, whose entire worldview is shaped by disdain for royalty and aversion to the monarchy. That's why he took such pleasure in my walk of shame."

"Walk of shame?" I ask, as I write that down in my notes. "Tell me about that."

"It is just as it is named. I was made to strip naked and walk the outskirts of the castle as the common people pelted me with rotten vegetables, all in an effort to force me to accept and acknowledge the actions I must feel shame for."

"That sounds like it was difficult."

"It was. It was intended to break me. To humiliate me. And in some sense it did, but I am too strong a person to ever lose faith in myself. Even if as part of the ruse I had to present myself as if I had. Accept my punishment, turn over a new leaf, all that. You see, I know from experience that if one is being tortured and wishes it to end, one must act as if the torture hurts. Defiance to torture only brings on more of the same."

"Sounds like you have some experience with torture," I observe.

"Oh, I do. Both as torturer and torturee." She grins wickedly. "The former is preferable."

"You know, shame is a tricky emotion. It can be relentless, and at the same time hidden. It can exist in the background of our lives, affecting everything we do and feel. But from what I'm hearing, you didn't feel it in this situation."

"I feel no shame, period. I am a queen," says Cersei defiantly. "It is impossible for me to be wrong about anything. Why should I feel shame?"

I shrug and don't respond. We sit there for a quiet moment. Then I think of a question.

"What did you do that this High Sparrow considered a sin?"

"I am accused of adultery."

"I see. A classic sin," I observe.

"Perhaps, but not worthy in my view of the punishment I have been assigned."

"Any other sins you've been accused of?"

Cersei opens her mouth to speak, then thinks better of it. "How do I know I can trust you?"

"Anything you say here is held in complete confidence, and

won't be shared with anyone outside this room without your permission."

"Anything?"

"Yes. With a few exceptions. I am a mandated reporter, so there are some things I am required to report if I hear them in session. These involve statements regarding harm to yourself, harm to others, and abuse of children or elders. Everything else is top secret."

Cersei nods, considering this, eyeing me intently. "And I see from your paperwork that you're a Stark. I am kin to some Starks, and I cannot say I trust them. Any relationship?"

"Not that I'm aware of. Also, no relation to Tony Stark."

"Tony Stark? I know not of that one."

"Iron Man. From the Avengers?"

Cersei looks at me quizzically, so I get back on track.

"My point is, anything you say here is in complete confidence, with a few exceptions that you're now aware of. So, you should feel free to share whatever you want without fear of it leaving this room."

"Very well. I have also been accused of regicide. This is related to the death of my first husband, Robert. He was such a boor. Ironically, he was killed by a boar." She chuckles.

"I see." I sit in silence and wait for her to continue. Cersei seems to be waiting for me to ask a follow up question, but I don't. Now she seems uncomfortable, and after a moment speaks up again.

"There is another sin."

I continue to sit in silence, looking at her, waiting.

"Do you wish to know it?" Cersei asks.

"Yes, if you're willing to share," I reply.

Cersei seems to consider what she's about to say, becoming more emotional now, more vulnerable. Then it all comes out in one big burst.

"I have an incestuous relationship with my twin brother Jaime, and have borne three children with him, passing them off as offspring of King Robert and keeping this a secret, thus creating a fraudulent line of succession to the throne of Westeros, and in theory the entire Seven Kingdoms and the Iron Throne."

I jot this information down in my notes. "The Iron Throne?"

"The seat of power over the whole of the known world."

"Sounds like a big deal," I say.

"Indeed, it is the biggest of deals." Cersei's affect has changed now. She seems looser, more relaxed. "I must say, it feels good to share this secret with someone I'm not related too. It feels like a burden lifted."

"I'm glad to hear that," I say. "It's amazing how powerful it can be to verbalize strong and repressed emotions we've been carrying around inside."

"Well said. So yes, that is the truth of the matter. Now, the High Sparrow suspected as much, but there was also evidence that I slept with a cousin, Lancel, because I did. But that was just about sex and obedience, with no implications for the bloodline. So I admitted to that, which satisfied the High Sparrow because it was still reason enough to punish me thus, so I have successfully avoided having to disclose any of this information with anyone outside of my family." She fixes a steely gaze on me. "Except for you."

"And my lips are sealed," I say, intimidated.

"Good." Cersei seems to have moved on past the emotions of this topic, and is ready for a new one. "I'm curious about why the Sparrow sought to have me attend therapy. Perhaps it's just something one is expected to do when being punished for their crimes. Perhaps my time here with you is supposed to help me see the error of my ways, and be inspired to change and act differently?"

“That’s often the case,” I say.

“That seems like the expectation, but it will not be the result. I have an indomitable will, a long memory, and I’m willing to play the game however I must in order to win.”

“And what is the game exactly?”

“The biggest game of them all. The game of power. You either win, or you die. And in the end, I shall be the victor.”

I sneak a look at the clock. “Well, we’re just about out of time for today. It’s noted in your paperwork that we’re to see each other seven more times.”

“Very well. Although I have a trial date next week, and if things go according to plan, I might not be back here at all.”

“Okay, well, just keep me updated.”

I rise as Cersei stands up and approaches the office door.

“Ser Gregor!” she calls.

From outside my office the door is opened by a gigantic, helmeted knight in metal armor.

“Maybe the gods go with you,” says Cersei, as they exit.

“And you have a great week,” I reply.

I close the door behind them, then sit down to write up my notes.

Clinical Notes: Client presented with a regal affect, even as her clothes and hair were dirty and disheveled. Client revealed her lack of enthusiasm for therapy, this being a process she was mandated to experience via court order. Client described events that led her to being incarcerated, and after confirming Therapist’s confidentiality policy, spoke about the crimes she committed, including details about the intersection of her family and romantic life. Client was resistant to therapy at first, but seemed to warm up as session progressed, and confirmed future attendance to seven more mandated sessions, although hinting at the possibility of upcoming events that might affect that schedule.

. . .

Diagnosis:

Z65.3: Problems Related to Legal Circumstances

Z63.8: Other Specified Problems Related to Primary Support Group

4

HARRY BURNS AND SALLY ALBRIGHT BURNS

Intake Information: Clients are a 36 year old male and a 35 year old female who have been married for two years, and seek therapy for help with conflict in their relationship. Clients describe a "storybook" relationship history over a long period of time, with alternating periods of close friendship and romantic attachment beginning early in their adult lives. Clients eventually reconnected later in life and got married, but after a relatively short period of time found themselves increasingly at odds. Clients are married with no children, and report having some previous therapy experience.

Harry Burns and Sally Albright Burns sit on the couch across from me, taking turns telling me the story of their relationship.

"So I go and run into the party and find her—" says Harry.

"Everyone's all dressed up formally and he runs in off the street like a crazy person—" interjects Sally.

"And I finally tell her I love her and I want to spend the rest of my life with her—"

"Which we'd talked about in the past but somehow it seemed much more real in that moment—"

"And I get real specific, like how I love that she gets cold when it's seventy one degrees outside, and it takes her an hour and a half to order a sandwich—"

"And I tell him I hate him but I love him, and I think I hate him because I love him so much—"

"So then I say that when you want to spend the rest of your life with someone, you want the rest of your life to start as soon as possible," says Harry.

"And he sweeps me off her feet, we go home, have the best sex of our lives, and three months later we're married," says Sally.

"And here we are now, in couples therapy," finishes Harry.

They finish their story and I sit there for a moment, thinking about what they've just told me, then offer my thoughts. "That's a remarkable relationship story. I can see why you described it as "storybook" in your intake paperwork."

Harry scoffs at this, while Sally grimaces. I jot down their reactions in my notes as I ask: "Do you still think of your relationship as storybook?"

"Maybe, but that story has ended," says Harry. "Now we're dealing with a different story from a different book that's not so enjoyable."

"I guess there's a reason we weren't a couple for all those years," observes Sally.

"Tell me more about your relationship now, and the things about it that have led you here," I say.

They look to each other. "Why don't you start, and if we have time left afterwards I'll go," says Harry.

Sally shakes her head, annoyed. "Fine. Harry has moments where he's this grand romantic, like that night at the New Year's eve party, where all he wants is me and he'll be happy in life. But when things get serious, more intimate, he pulls away. And this is a perfect example: a grand gesture, totally romantic, then we get married and move in together, and a couple of months later he becomes cold and distant. It's all fun and games when he's chasing me down, but once we're in a committed relationship and it's time to start dealing with the realities of married life, like planning summer vacations or figuring out how to decorate the bedroom, he checks out. He just shuts down. I think he's scared of intimacy."

I sit and wait after Sally finishes, waiting to see if she'll continue and how Harry will react. Harry speaks first.

"Thanks for giving us the short version."

"You're welcome."

I turn to Harry. "What's your version?"

"My version? My version is the flip side of that. I'm just living my life, like I've always been, but somehow the things I do drive her crazy now. Even more, I should say. What does it matter if the eight pillows on the bed aren't arranged correctly? And more importantly, why does me not caring about that send her into this spiral where one minute we're talking about pillows and the next she's questioning our relationship? And then, instead of yelling or arguing, I tell her I need my space, in a very clear and non-threatening way, but instead of giving me that space, she follows me around the apartment, and if I leave to go for a walk she's calling me asking where I am and when I'm going to be home, and then she starts in with how we need therapy to work on our relationship." He turns to Sally. "Sound about right?"

"Yep, that's our relationship in a nutshell," says Sally, who then turns to me. "So, what do you think, Phil? Is there hope for us?"

"Oh, there's hope for everyone. But we don't have to rely on hope. At a certain point in a relationship, it takes work to make things the way you want them to be. It takes work to change, which is not something most people are want to do. And I think what you're describing, this dynamic between you, this push and pull, is a common dynamic in relationships. Have you guys ever heard of the idea of Attachment Styles?"

"I loved their first album," jokes Harry.

"Can you please take this seriously?" asks Sally.

I ignore this and continue.

"There's a particular modality of couples therapy that deals with the concept of Attachment Styles. This is the idea that we each have a psychological blueprint that shapes how we experience intimacy in adult relationships. A common situation is when one person can be described as having an anxious attachment style, and the other an avoidant attachment style. In a very broad sense, this dynamic plays out when the anxious partner feels some sort of distance or conflict in their relationship, and their reaction is to reach out for assurance, to draw closer. And the avoidant partner's reaction to relationship conflict is to want their space, to pull away. Which leads the anxious one to reach out more, which causes the avoidant one to pull away more. Now, that's a very broad description of the theory, and it's not like I'm diagnosing you with this, but do you guys identify with that at all?"

Harry and Sally answer at the same time: "Yes. / Absolutely."

"Okay, good. Then let's run with that. Tell me, can you think of a specific issue in your relationship that fits into this framework?"

"The pillows," Harry says instantly. "She has this way of arranging the pillows on the bed, which is fine, whatever, but if I do anything to disturb them she reacts like she caught me cheating on her. She can't let it go. I just don't get why it's such a big deal."

"The thing is—" Sally starts to responds, but I interrupt.

"Hold that thought, Sally. Let's let Harry have the floor and I'll give you a chance to respond afterwards."

I turn back to Harry. "Harry, I understand what you're saying. Especially the part about not getting why it's such a big deal to Sally. But here's the thing: I suspect you will never get why it's such a big deal to her. And I bet that no matter how many times she's explained it to you, you just don't get it, and you never will."

"Hallelujah!" exclaims Harry.

"So here's something to think about," I continue. "Trying to get it and not being able to is a road block to the kind of relationship happiness most people want. The trick, Harry, is being able to accept that there are things about Sally you don't get, and you will never get. But if you can learn to accept these things you don't get, to eliminate them as starting points for conflict, you can get past them and start being happier in the relationship. Basically, the challenge is to get over having to get it."

Harry nods, considering this while I turn to Sally.

"Okay Sally, tell me your take on the pillow situation."

"I just like things the way I like them," she says. "I have a specific way I want our bedroom to look. And when I ask him to support me in this, he makes me feel like a crazy person, like I'm asking him to run a marathon instead of just not leave the bed looking like a war zone."

"They're just pillows!" explodes Harry.

This outburst of anger surprises us all. I let the words hang for a moment, then chime in. "It feels like we're talking about more than just pillows here. And Sally, I'll bet that you just don't get why Harry can't do something as simple as not mess up the pillows."

"You're right, I don't."

"And no matter how many times you've explained it to him, he just doesn't get it."

"He doesn't."

"So, the idea here is to get over having to get it. Because you've given it every chance. I don't know if there's a way to explain things in a way that you will each understand and appreciate. No minds are going to be changed here. I think learning to accept the things about each other you don't get will open you up to enjoying each other's company in all the good ways that you've already experienced without things like the pillow situation getting you stuck in this cycle of conflict."

"So what, I have to just sit and watch him dismiss my

pillows?" Sally says, frustrated. "Because when he does that, it feels like he's dismissing me."

I lean forward to agree with her. "Exactly! It feels like he's dismissing you when he dismisses the pillows, but he's really just dismissing the pillows. So the challenge for you is to understand that when he dismisses the pillows, he's not dismissing you, and to not react like he is."

Then I turn to Harry. "And the challenge for you is to understand that when you dismiss the pillows, Sally feels like you're dismissing her, even if that's the furthest thing from your mind."

They both sit there, considering all this.

"Does all that make sense?" I ask.

"Yeah," says Harry. "It just sounds like a lot of challenges."

"I agree, it does. But this is where relationships end up when we get past the storybook phase. This is when we get into what people call 'the work', which I think means the approach of changing your actions and attitude to accommodate the needs and feelings of your partner. And if both people are trying to treat the other the way they want to be treated, both people will be happy."

"Theoretically," repeats Harry.

"Yes," I continue. "Now with you guys, that might look something like this: Harry acknowledges that even though he doesn't get Sally's thing about the pillows, he accepts that she feels the way she does, and he puts some effort into doing things in a way Sally will appreciate, whether that means putting the pillows back in the right order or just not complaining about them, or whatever. And for Sally, this might look like understanding that Harry doesn't get her approach to the pillows, and that sometimes he's not going to do the pillow thing the way she wants, but instead of escalating things in those moments she can instead let this instinct pass, and prevent it from creating conflict."

They both think about this for a moment, digesting.

"It makes sense when you say it," observes Sally.

Harry agrees. "Yeah, can you write that down for us?"

"I think you guys have plenty to chew on, and I'm sure you'll have chances over the next week to work on this. In fact, I'm pretty sure those pillows are waiting on your bed right now, so you'll get to try this new approach to that discussion as early as tonight."

"Oh, I know those pillows are waiting for us, all piled up in a pillow tower," says Harry.

Sally looks annoyed, but Harry reaches out and takes her hand. "I'm sorry, I don't mean to hurt your feelings. I'm going to try harder about the pillows."

Sally is touched. "Thank you. So will I."

I appreciate this moment, and want to reflect that to them. "Well, in terms of a couples therapy session, that's a storybook ending! Now, we're just about out of time for today, but I'm looking forward to hearing about your experiences next week, pillow-related and otherwise."

I stand up and cross over to open the office door for them.

"I'm starving. Wanna go to Katz's?" Harry asks Sally. "If we call in your order we could save fifteen minutes."

"You joke, but that's a good idea," says Sally. "I'll call from the car. What do you want?"

"I'll have what you're having," replies Harry.

"Excellent choice."

They share a quick, tender kiss, then exit.

I close the door behind them, then sit down to write up my notes.

Clinical Notes: Clients presented with engaged affects, both describing a dynamic that Therapist related to their possible Attachment Styles. Clients described a relationship history with ups and downs that led to a declaration of love and marriage, but after a short period of time consistent conflict has become a feature of their relationship. Therapist worked with Clients to identify the frustration they feel when their parter does not 'get' them, and instead learn to accept the things about their partner they do not get. The experience of Sally's preference with pillows, and Harry inability to understand this, was used as an example to illustrate this dynamic, and Clients intend to approach this situation next with a hopefully different result.

Diagnosis:

Z63.0: Relationship Distress with Spouse or Partner

5

WALTER WHITE

Intake Information: Client is a 50 year old male who seeks therapy for support after recently receiving a terminal cancer diagnosis. Client describes this news as "crushing," and also considers his deteriorating financial position and added strain of a second child on the way as contributing to growing feelings of hopelessness and depression. Client reports feeling stunned and numb by recent events in his life, and has come to therapy for help navigating these issues. Client is married, has one child, is expecting another, and reports no previous therapy experience.

Walter White sits on the couch across from me in silence, dressed in rumpled khakis and a beige windbreaker. He looks beaten down and numb, staring off into the distance in an unfocused way. I sit in the uncomfortable silence with him.

After a long moment, he finally speaks. "So, what do we do here?"

"Well, we usually talk about the issues that bring us to therapy. However, sometimes those issues can be so big that we might just sit here and process them. Try to make sense of them, figure out how to react to them. That seems like what we're doing now."

I watch as Walter nods and thinks about this. I give him some space to reply, but he doesn't, so I continue.

"I mean, you've just received a scary diagnosis. Stage four lung cancer. In your intake paperwork you use words like "inoperable" and "terminal." We can't expect to just take that news in and go on about our day without some kind of reaction. And the bigger the shock, the longer the news might take to process."

Walter sits there, still taking it all in. Then he squints and looks closer at me.

"What's that stain on your shirt?" he asks.

I look down at a tiny yellow dried drop of mustard.

"Oh, that's a bit of mustard from lunch. Great cheeseburgers at the taco stand down the street, if you like cheeseburgers."

Walter nods, then sighs loudly. "Lung cancer. Terminal. Inoperable. It's amazing how much these words have the power to turn my life upside down. Not that it was going so well right side up."

"How long ago did you get this news?"

"A week. But here I am, still walking around in a daze, like I don't know what to do with myself. How long does this last? This feeling of... emptiness?"

"I don't know. But I think talking about it here will help shorten that period, or at least help in the processing of the experience."

"I haven't cried. Is that normal?" Walter asks.

"It's normal to react the way you're reacting," I say. "You've just had a traumatic experience, getting some scary news, and it makes sense your reaction is to shut down. Some people wail and cry and emote, some people withdraw and go numb."

"Numb. That's a good word. That's how I feel. That and angry."

"Tell me about the anger."

Walter sits up, becoming engaged now. "I'm angry that this happened to me. I don't deserve cancer. I don't deserve a death sentence. But I also didn't deserve a lot of things that have happened to me. Things with school, with work, with relationships... I've been getting screwed over my whole life."

"Tell me about some of the ways you've gotten screwed over."

"Well, I'm thinking specifically of a business venture that could have made me a millionaire. Gray Matter Technologies. You've heard of them, right?"

"Sorry, I haven't."

"That's fine, it's just a billion dollar company that a close friend and I started, built on my research and scientific findings. But the trouble was more about a relationship I was in. That I was scared of. With someone involved with the company. So I bailed on it. The relationship. Which led to me bailing on the company. I took a five thousand dollar payout that would be worth five million right now if I'd stayed."

"And how did you get screwed?"

Walter considers this. "I guess I didn't really get screwed. I screwed myself. I was scared. I felt small and powerless, and I acted in an immature, childish way to get myself out of the situation. I certainly could have handled it better. And if I had I definitely wouldn't find myself in the situation I am now, teaching high school chemistry to kids who don't care making peanuts a day and unable to support my family in the way they deserve."

Walter leans back on the couch, letting this all sink in. "I think about it every day. How things could have been different. I mean, with work and finances and all. Not the cancer. I supposed that was unavoidable. Unless years of regret and jealousy can cause cancer. Can they?"

"I don't know. I think we should assume that the cancer was unavoidable. The feelings of jealousy and regret we can work with."

Walter continues, on a roll. "I know I've had these feelings my whole life, and I've been carrying them around but pushing them down, they've been running in the background, but still there. Always there. And this cancer news was a spark that lit those old emotions back on fire."

"You know, I often hear clients talk about the regrets they have in life, and how they would like to have done things differently. To have reacted to certain news differently, to have handled a situation differently, to have taken a different course of action. Some of them end up making the changes or taking the actions in the present that they wish they had taken in the past, and after they've done that, almost every one of them said to me some version of "I thought it was too late, but it turns out it wasn't."

Walter looks at me, unconvinced. "Is that supposed to be inspiring?"

"It's not supposed to be anything. It's just an experience that I wanted to share with you because I think it applies to your situation."

Walter seems annoyed. "Were any of those clients recently diagnosed with Stage III Bronchogenic Carcinoma?"

"No. It's more common for me to hear clients talk about regrets and it being too late in terms of relationship conflict or career struggles. Your situation is certainly more—"

"Life or death," Walter interrupts. "And trending towards death. I know I can't go back and change how I acted, or what I did. I can certainly continue to torture myself about it, but that's not going to change the predicament I find myself in, I know that. But I guess I should start thinking about what I can do now. What I can do now to change what's happening right now, instead of feeling like a sad sack for what I could have done in the past."

"Yes!" I'm excited to hear Walter say this, but try to stop myself from getting too enthusiastic. "I think that's exactly the kind of attitude that will help as you deal with what's going on right now and what you can do in this moment, instead of ruminating on what happened in the past, and what you could have done back then."

Walter looks like he's got more of a spark now. "Somehow this news of impending death makes me want to finally be more proactive in life."

Walter takes out a piece of paper from his jacket pocket and unfolds it.

"I've run the numbers and determined that, in order for my wife, son, and unborn child to be somewhat comfortable financially going forward after my death, they're going to need seven hundred and thirty seven thousand dollars."

"That's pretty specific," I observe. "How did you come up with that number?"

"It's the combination of mortgage debt, cost of living, educational outlays, and other assorted expenses."

"Seven hundred and thirty seven. You didn't want to just round that to seven hundred and forty?"

Walter gets serious. "I'm a scientist. I don't round." Then he looks back down at the number on the piece of paper. "You know, it's funny, but this death sentence is starting to make me more focused on life than I've ever been."

"It sounds like you're changing from thinking about what you could have done in the past, which is out of your hands, to what you can do now, which is within your power."

"Exactly. At first I was sad, but now I'm inspired. Shouldn't I be, like, grieving?"

"That's an interesting question," I observe. "In therapy we often deal with grief. This is usually thought of as the experience we have after someone passes away. But there are many kinds of grief, including anticipatory grief. That's something we can experience when a loved one has a terminal disease that forces us to reckon with the idea that they'll soon be dead even as they're still alive. And this gives us a chance to take action regarding an event that hasn't happened yet."

"So that's what I have, this anticipatory grief, only it's about myself?"

"I think that concept could apply here. I mean, It's different for everyone. Some people find themselves stuck, unable to act, until the anticipation of death leads to the actual death. Some people, on the other hand, find themselves compelled to act, to do the things they might want to do now that, if not for this anticipatory period, they would regret not having done after their loved one dies. Or they do."

"I see. Yes, that certainly puts a name to what I'm feeling," says Walter. "I do feel like I want to act. Like I need to act. I just don't know what the action is yet."

"That can be an upside of anticipatory grief. The event that will eventually cause the actual grief hasn't happened yet, so there's still time to, if not change the outcome, change the experience leading up to it."

Walter nods, sitting up straighter, his mood more upbeat now. "Yeah. I like that. It does make me feel a little better. Like, it's motivating me to get off my butt and do something. I just wish I could have felt like this years ago, before the diagnosis."

"Yes, well, life is full of ironies."

"It is indeed."

Walter's watch alarm goes off.

"Sorry, I'm going to have to cut this short. I have to get back to school for a meeting with a student. When are we set to meet next?"

"Same time next week. Also, we discussed the possibility of a psychiatric referral to see if anti-depressant medication was something you might benefit from. Would you like that referral?"

"No thanks, I'm not into drugs. But I'll reach back out if that changes."

I rise and open the office door for him.

"No problem. Good luck!"

Walter exits, and I close the door behind him, then sit down to write up my notes.

Clinical Notes: Client presented with a flat affect, dealing with the aftereffects of a terminal cancer diagnosis. Client regrets choices he's made in the past regarding his career, and wishes he was better able to support his family financially, especially in light of new information regarding his health. Time was spent processing this regret, and how holding on to it has prevented Client from taking action to change his life in the present. Therapist and Client discussed anticipatory grief, how Client is experiencing this regarding his own possible death, the idea of regrets in life, and the possibility for Client to take actions now to mitigate that regret. Client exhibited a change in affect after this discussion, and ended session remarking on how he felt better.

Diagnosis:

F43.21: Adjustment Disorder with Depressed Mood

Z71.85: Encounter for Anticipatory Grief

6

BERTHA RUSSELL

Intake Information: Client is a 41 year old female seeking therapy for support regarding conflict with her daughter. Client has arranged for daughter's marriage to someone she considers to be a desirable partner, but daughter does not share this sentiment. This has created significant tension between Client and daughter, and Client also notes that this conflict has negatively affected relationship with husband and son. Client specifically noted in intake paperwork a desire for help "convincing daughter to see things my way." Client is married with two children, and indicates no previous therapy experience.

Bertha Russell sits on the couch across from me, wearing an elaborate dress with a large, colorful hat, and a closed parasol leans against the couch next to her. Her posture is proper, and she smoothes down her dress as she speaks.

"I specifically chose you because you are a man," says Bertha. "I just don't see how a woman would be qualified to do the work of a doctor."

"Actually, I'm not a doctor."

Bertha looks concerned. "Excuse me?"

"I have a master's degree in Psychology, but I didn't go to medical school," I say. "But I assure you, I'm fully qualified and trained to work as a therapist."

"I see," Bertha says, considering this. "Well, I hope you can help me either way, doctor or not. My point is, there are some things women are simply not capable of, and acting as an authority on matters of medicine and mental health is one of them. I find the majority of women to be weak and spineless. Unlike me. I've always been told I carry myself like a man."

"In what way?"

Bertha considers this. "Well, I'm confident. I know what I want and I go out and get it. I don't just sit back and wait for a man to do things for me. Unless that's what I prefer in the moment."

"Those seem to be admirable qualities for any gender," I observe.

"I agree. I hope my daughter will grow up to be like me. A woman with a spine, with intellect, with force of will. I'm just afraid that if she continues to resist my support she'll end up like all the others."

"What others?"

"Oh, the various daughters of women in my social circle. They're all of the same class, I suppose, with similar ranks in society, and similar paths available to them. But they are doomed to lead quiet, boring lives of mediocrity. I want something else for Gladys. I want her to achieve great things. That's why this marriage is so important."

"Yes, the marriage. I read about this in your intake paperwork, but why don't you give me the broad strokes?" I ask.

"Simply put, I've arranged for Gladys to marry the Duke of Buckingham. And this was not easy, by any means. It look all of my planning, my resources, my cunning. She'll be a noble! An aristocrat. She'll have a title. My daughter, the Duchess of Buckingham." Bertha sighs with contentment. "Doesn't that sound wonderful?"

I choose not to answer the question. "How does Gladys feel about this plan?"

Bertha's mood shifts instantly from happiness to annoyance.

"She's being such a child about it. She refuses to appreciate the practical aspects of this match. The opportunities that will be available to her. She's got this idea that she might marry for love," Bertha says with a scoff. "Which might work for other people, for common people. But for us, at the top tier of society, it doesn't work like that."

"And she's made clear to you her resistance to this arrangement?"

"She has. But with time I trust she'll eventually appreciate the lengths I went to to give her this opportunity."

"You also mentioned in your intake paperwork that your husband and son are not in favor of this arrangement?"

Bertha waves her hand dismissively. "Oh, my husband will come around. He's nothing if not practical. He can certainly appreciate the financial implications of this pairing, even if it will certainly cost him a pretty penny. And while expensive, this arrangement will be a business expense for him, an investment, and he understands that it will help raise his stature in society and commerce, which will be a positive influence on his future business dealings, especially internationally. Now, my son? He's naive. He too believes in "love." He even thinks his infatuation with the neighbor girl across the street is a secret from me. But I have my spies."

"Is this relationship with the neighbor serious? I mean, is he considering marriage as well?"

"He thinks he is, but I know better. I would consider giving him a chance to marry for love, as long as the match meets my financial and social expectations. And the neighbor girl does not. Oh, she's fine to have over for tea and is pleasant enough at a dinner party, but she doesn't have the proper lineage to be a match for my son." Bertha sighs. "I must tell you, it is difficult being a mother."

"I can only imagine. But I can relate to the work of being a parent. What was your relationship like with your parents?"

Bertha seems surprised to be asked this question. “My parents? What do they have to do with this?”

“Well, I find that when discussing our relationships with our children, it can often be helpful to examine our relationship with our parents to see how our past might influence what we’re experiencing in the present.”

Bertha seems skeptical, but game. “Very well. My father was a potato farmer. That tells you everything you need to know right there.”

“I’m sorry, I don’t know much about potato farming,” I admit.

“What is there to know?” Bertha says, annoyed. “It’s a lower class occupation. It’s certainly not a respected career. In fact, it was embarrassing. Seeing him come home with dirt on his hands, mud on his clothes, unable to afford the things we wanted. And my mother, with her thoughts forever destined to be focused on mundane tasks like cooking and cleaning, unable to free her mind to enjoy anything resembling society, or the arts. It was clear to me from an early age that I aspired to more. And marrying well was an important factor in that process.”

“How did you meet your husband?”

Bertha smiles as she reminisces. “The old fashioned way, in the street. He wasn’t well bred but he was ambitious. When we met he was a young engineer, and he had grand aspirations, which made him extremely attractive to me. I could tell he was destined to be rich. And I chose well, as he went on to found one of the nation’s leading railroad companies, and become richer than we could have ever imagined. And while he was working hard at building his business, I was working hard at building our reputation, our place in society. That was hard work as well. I honestly don’t know who had the harder job.”

“So, your marriage wasn’t a match based on money or social stature?” I ask.

“It was not, but don’t try to paint me as a hypocrite,” says

Bertha, suspicious now. "Generations differ in their opportunities and limitations, and we can only live with the options our time in life presents us with. But more importantly, let's address the reason I've sought your advice: How can you help me change my daughter's mind? To see things my way?"

I nod as I consider this. "Yes, that's a good question. Unfortunately, I can't do that. But tell me this: If your daughter were sitting here with me instead of you, what do you think she'd say about the situation?"

Bertha laughs. "She'd say her mother is a mean old warhorse who's making her do something she doesn't want to."

"And your husband?"

"He'd say I should back off and give Gladys a chance to meet a man she loves while hoping that it turns out he's a match I might approve of."

"And your son?"

"He'd tell you how angry he is that I've made his sister this match, and perhaps admit his fear that I plan the same for him. Which I do."

"So, it sounds like all the people in your family want different outcomes than you."

"Exactly. And they're all wrong," Bertha says defiantly.

"I can appreciate that you want me to help you convince your family to feel the way you do, but that's not something I can do. In fact, my work with you on this topic might actually achieve the opposite. Meaning, we would attempt to develop an appreciation for the needs and desires of the other people in your life, and try to learn to accept them, even if they're contrary to our own."

Bertha listens to this, and fixes me with a steely glare. "Well, that simply won't do. I've put in too much time and effort into this arrangement to simply let my daughter do what she wants." Then Bertha seems to come up with a new idea in the moment.

"Might I send them to you? Could you guide them to see the error of their ways?"

I ignore the question. "Do you think your husband's disagreement with you about this marriage might cause further conflict between you?"

It seems like this is something Bertha has already considered. "I have to admit that is a fear. I've seen George take a stand on other issues, but eventually come around. This time, however, there's something different about his reaction. He seems to be taking this more seriously." Bertha has become pensive, but quickly shakes it off. "But he'll get used to it. Just like he did the ballroom, and the opera house, and all the other things I was right about."

"And how do you think your son will react if this marriage ends up happening?"

"Oh, this marriage will be happening. Now, what happens if he wants to marry some commoner and I don't approve? Well, that would be a different story. I assume he'd threaten to elope, we'd inform him that he'd be disowned and have no financial support from us, he'd rebel against us in some immature way, then see the folly of his childish actions, and come back around to the match we desire for him."

"You know Bertha, it sounds like the things you want for your children, the social status and financial situation, these are things you wanted when you were younger."

"They certainly were. And now I want them for my children."

"But it sounds like they don't want them."

"Obviously, but what do they know?" says Bertha, frustrated. "They're children!"

"They're also people who might be considered by some to be young adults. Or just plain adults, even. Capable of making their own decisions about the way they want to live their lives."

"Excuse me?" Bertha seems offended. "That point of view is in direct contradiction to everything I've just told you."

"I know. And I apologize if it's unpleasant to be disagreed with, but sometimes my job is to present the opposing point of view."

"Well, I don't intend to sit here and listen to you argue against my position. I'll simply pay you and be on my way." With that, she gathers her things and rises, as do I.

"Your advertisement was misspelled to say your fee is two hundred and fifty dollars, so here is your correct compensation," she says, as she takes some coins out of her wallet and puts them on the coffee table. "I'm sure you meant two dollars and fifty cents."

"Actually, that wasn't a typo," I say.

Bertha looks shocked. "Two hundred and fifty dollars? Even I don't carry that kind of money around. No matter, I'll send my footman by with payment tomorrow."

"I'd appreciate that. And you know, you don't have to leave. We still have some time left, we could continue the conversation."

"I'm not interested. I'd rather find a therapist who is intelligent enough to agree with me."

"Very well then," I say, as I open the office door for her.

"Thank you for your time, Doctor. Oh wait, you're not a doctor. My mistake."

She grins devilishly as she exits.

I close the door behind her, then sit down to write up my notes.

Clinical Notes: Client presented with a focused affect, clear-minded about her goals for therapy, which seem to be to convince the people in her life to act in the way that she sees fit. Client has arranged a marriage for her daughter that she considers optimal in terms of social fit, but daughter does not want this. Neither do Client's husband and son. Client showed frustration when told by Therapist that he would not be able to convince her family to change their minds, and that instead the change would have to come from Client. Client terminated session early.

Diagnosis:

Z62.820: Parent-Biological Child Conflict
Z63.0: Relationship Distress with Spouse or Partner

7

THE AVENGERS

Intake Information: Clients are four coworkers: TS, SR, BB, and TO. Clients are aged respectively 53, 105, 54, and 1521, and while TS is married, the others are single. Clients seek therapy because of continued conflict that occurs in the course of their work together. They describe their work as intense and important, yet with all the exterior forces they find themselves battling against, they identify the conflict between TS and SR as their main source of frustration, with this frustration bubbling over into other aspects of their relationships. Clients state they hope to mitigate this conflict in order to understand and support each other better, and to be able to focus on their work.

My office feels smaller today as there are four large, muscular men joining me, three squeezed together on the couch and another on a chair to the side.

Tony, well groomed and wearing an expensive looking suit, sits on one side of the couch.

Steve, wearing unremarkable casual clothes, sits on the other side.

Bruce sits between them, wearing a white lab coat.

Thor is in a chair off to the side, dressed in shiny armor, a large steel hammer on the ground by his side.

"Nice setup you got here," observes Tony. "Where do you keep the shrunken heads?"

"Give it a rest, Tony. This isn't the place to be cracking jokes," says Steve, annoyed.

"I don't know, it seems like the perfect place," replies Tony, who then turns to me. "Wouldn't you agree, Phil?"

I shrug, trying to stay out of it. "For some people, humor is a way to reduce tension."

"Exactly, thank you," says Tony, satisfied.

"Or to distract from more serious issues," I add.

Steve nods approvingly. "My thoughts exactly."

Bruce leans forward from his spot between them. "Can we please not start with this? I'm sick of being stuck in the middle of all your snarky back-and-forths."

"Right," I observe. "It's interesting, Bruce, that you spoke in your intake paperwork about feeling like you always have to be the referee between Tony and Steve, and here you are sitting literally right between them."

"Hey, nobody asked him to be the referee," says Tony.

"Somebody has to be," Bruce says. "Here we are, constantly trying to save the planet, or even the universe, yet I find it actually more difficult to keep the peace between you two."

I sit with the moment as the men grumble in silent dissatisfaction, then speak up. "Am I correct in assuming this interaction is emblematic of the experience you're here to address?"

Tony points at me. "Ding ding ding, give that man a prize."

I look over to Thor, sitting on a chair apart from the others.

"Why don't you tell me what you think we're doing here, Thor?" I ask.

Thor, who had been playing distractedly with a tassel on his armor, looks up, surprised to be engaged. "What do I think? Well, Tony and Steve are like brothers who never get along. They're constantly arguing and can't agree on anything, which makes our work extremely difficult, since a lot of the job entails coming up with a plan everyone can agree on, and overall I'd say their relationship has become a major distraction."

I turn to the others. "Do the rest of you feel like that's accurate?"

They nod in agreement, and I continue.

"I like how you used the word brothers, Thor, because even though you're not related, you've come together to form a group, and each of you functions within the group in the same way family members do. A family dynamic can develop out of work relationships. You're a work family."

Tony agrees. "Like a band. Did you see that Metallica documentary? Something about a monster? Where they go to therapy?"

"Some Kind of Monster," says Thor.

"Right, it's called something something monster," agrees Tony.

"No, that's the title, Some Kind of Monster," Thor replies, annoyed. "You never listen to me."

"I did see that movie," I share. "And to be honest, whenever I pitch this take on work relationships in group settings, someone mentions it."

Tony leans forward, engaged. "I'm not even the biggest Metallica fan and I found it pretty interesting. The way that Lars kept acting like—"

Steve interrupts him, annoyed. "I'm sorry, but can we stick to the work family that's in this room at the moment?"

Now Tony sits back, annoyed. "You're such a sour puss."

"You're such a child."

"I know you are but what am I?

Bruce slams his hand on the coffee table. "Will you two please give it a rest? You're making me angry!"

Bruce suddenly starts to shudders and groan.

"Great, now look what you did!" Bruce says as he grimaces, and then swiftly transforms into a muscular green person twice his original size.

I look on at this transformation, trying to keep my composure. “Are you okay, Bruce?”

Even though Bruce has now transformed into a huge, muscular, green-skinned hulk, his voice and affect are the same as before. “I’m fine, this is just what happens when I get mad. Which, as you might suspect, is happening a lot lately.”

I pick back up the thread of the session. “Okay. Well, speaking of the family dynamic, it seems like you’re the one playing the role of the caretaking parent in this family, Bruce, trying to make sure everyone gets along, stuck in the middle, sometimes quite literally.”

Thor speaks up, now more engaged. “That’s Bruce alright, acting like everyone’s mom, trying to make sure everyone gets along. Which is noble, but it ends up coming off as nagging. And honestly? It’s almost as annoying as the arguing.”

Bruce looks hurt. “Oh really? Well, if we’re a family, then you’re the black sheep younger brother who spends all his time in his room, never talks at dinner, and then goes off to college and never comes back.”

Now Thor’s the one who looks annoyed. “Oh great, this again.”

“Yeah, this again,” replies Bruce. “Because what we’re really here to talk about is everything that happened while you were missing in action."

“Well excuse me, but I had some very important stuff to deal with.”

“Oh right, that whole Ragnarok thing,” Tony chimes in.

“You could have called,” says Steve.

“I was busy!” Thor exclaims, now fully engaged in the conversation. “Fine, I’m so sorry that I had to leave Earth for a few years to take care of a little thing called *the death of the gods!*”

I try to take control of the conversation. “Okay, let’s stop for a second to take a deep breath and calm down. I mean literally. Let's all take some deep breaths in through the nose, hold for a moment, then exhale through the mouth."

I breathe in this way, and reluctantly the group follows my lead. After a couple of breaths the mood of the room seems to improve.

"Okay, good. Now, let's dive back in to the details of what specifically brought you guys here today. Tell me about…" I read from my notes. "Segovia?"

"Sokovia," says Steve. "You're familiar with that whole situation, right?"

"Not really. Catch me up."

Tony looks surprised. "Catch you up? That was big news. Sokovia? Age of Ultron? They made movies about it. Haven't you seen them?"

I shrug sheepishly. "Sorry, I'm more of a sports and news guy."

Steve leans in to explain. "Sokovia was a small Eastern European nation that served as a secret base for HYDRA experimentation that was tragically destroyed during a battle between the Avengers and Ultron, as a result of…"

Steve trails off as he looks towards Tony, who is staring off in the other direction.

Steve stops talking, now apologetic. "Sorry, Tony."

Tony shrugs, acting as if he's not hurt. "It's okay, you can say it. It was my fault."

"I wasn't going to say that," says Steve.

Now Tony lashes out in anger. "Oh thank you so much, you weren't going to say it? But you are going to make sure to tell me that you weren't going to say it, so actually that's just as good as saying it."

Now Bruce chimes in. "As a result of the Sokovia incident came the Sokovia accords, where some of us," he motions towards Tony, "wanted to cede more authority for our actions to the government, while others," he motions towards Steve, "wanted to keep complete autonomy over our work."

I nod, taking this in. "And is that the major point of contention between Tony and Steve?"

"We have to think about the endgame here," Tony says passionately. "If we don't submit to some kind of oversight we'll be viewed as vigilantes, or worse, terrorists. And what happened in Sokovia could happen again."

"It could happen again no matter what we do," says Steve, just as passionate. "I don't trust the government to make better decisions that we can. I mean, just look at SHIELD! Whoever would have thought that it would become HYDRA?"

Thor chimes in. "I had my suspicions."

"Tony, what about this is your fault?" I ask.

Tony sighs, his shoulders slump. "Sokovia happened because of Ultron, which was my creation. I bypassed safety protocols and didn't check with my teammates because I assumed I was smart enough to handle it. But it turns out I couldn't. So all that destruction, all those lives lost... That's on me."

"And do you feel guilty about that?"

Tony looks offended. "That's an obvious question."

"It is, and I apologize if that's annoying, but part of my job is to ask the obvious questions."

Tony continues. "Of course I feel guilty."

"Which you mask with your flippant remarks and cutting humor," says Bruce.

"Along with my vast wealth and good looks," says Tony.

"But it seems to me like some of that guilt gets transformed into anger," I observe. "And it clearly comes out in your interactions with Steve."

"Another genius observation," says Tony, annoyed.

I turn to Steve. "Can you see how the anger that Tony

responds to you with might be rooted in his feelings of guilt about the events in Sokovia?"

Tony nods, affirmative. "Of course, but what I'm trying to—"

"Hold on. Sorry to interrupt, but I'd like you to try not to use the word 'but.' When we talk to our partners in relationships about issues like this, things that make us emotional, and we say something and then qualify it by saying 'but,' well… Everything we say after the 'but' gets cancelled out."

Steve looks a bit confused. "Okay."

"So, let's try again. Steve, can you see how sometimes when you and Tony get into it, the anger he's directing at you might more about his feelings of guilt, and not necessarily caused by you?"

"Yes," Steve says. I can tell he wants to say 'but,' to share his reasons why, but he bites his tongue. I let the moment sit for a beat, then continue.

"Great. Now Steve, I'd like to hear more about your feelings about this SHIELD / HYDRA situation."

Steve gets serious. "I sacrificed a lot to stop HYDRA, and I spent my whole career fighting them alongside SHIELD. Then I come to find out that HYDRA had actually taken control of SHIELD. I can't tell you how much of a betrayal that was. I'll never trust them again."

"And what have you done with these feelings of betrayal?"

"What do you mean?"

"I mean, how have those feelings caused you to act?"

"Like a freaking maniac! There's no way in hell I'm ever signing those Sokovia Accords."

"I can feel the passion in your voice as you talk about this. And I can also see how this passion can turn so easily into anger as you interact with Tony. Can you see that, Tony?"

"Duh, it's obvious," says Tony.

"It does seem obvious, but we often avoid engaging with the obvious reasons behind our conflicts because of our own emotional material that we bring to the conversation. We often say we don't want to be angry and fight with each other, but I think deep down it feels good to be angry, it's satisfying somehow, so we give in to it. Anger can feel good."

"That's very true," says Bruce.

I sit with the group in the silence, letting what's been said sink in.

After a minute or so, Tony speaks up. "So, are we cured?"

"No," I say. "But you're on the path to healing."

"The path to healing," Thor repeats. "Sounds like a street in Asgard."

"I think you're starting to make changes for the better. What we tried to do here is have Tony and Steve understand more about each other's strong feelings, and how easily they can turn into anger at each other. This understanding is one small pebble in the river, but if we keep at it, keep throwing tiny pebbles in the river with conversations like this, eventually they accumulate enough to form a bridge to the other side. And what's on the other side?"

"Valhalla?" ventures Thor.

I look at Tony and Steve. "I'm asking you two. What's on the other side of that bridge?"

Tony and Steve eye each other warily.

"Peace?" says Tony.

"Understanding," says Steve.

"Everybody getting along," Bruce adds.

"I think those are all admirable goals. It sounds like you'd all like to get along better, right?"

Everyone nods and grumbles in agreement.

Good," I continue. "During the next week I want all of you to try to focus on moments when you would normally react with anger to each other, and instead try to make the moment less about getting angry and more about understanding each other.

Understanding *why* you're angry. And supporting each other in those moments. Does that sound doable?"

"It sounds hard, but we've done harder things," says Tony. "How many times have we saved the universe?"

"Which one?" replies Steve.

I sneak a look at the clock. "Well, we're just about out of time for today, so we'll have to pick back up here next week."

I stand up and cross over to open the office door for the group as they file out.

"So we are like Metallica," observes Thor.

"We are nothing like Metallica," Steve says, annoyed.

"We could be, but you're not cool enough to be in a band," says Tony.

"Shut up," responds Steve.

They exit, and I close the door behind them, then sit down to write up my notes, when I notice Thor has forgotten his hammer.

Before I can say anything the hammer rises up on its own and flies through the air, smashing through my office door, and into the hand of Thor, who stands in the hallway.

"Sorry about that. We'll Zelle you," says Thor sheepishly.

"We?" exclaims Bruce.

They continue to bicker as they leave, leaving me to contemplate the hole in my office door.

Clinical Notes: Clients presented with frustrated affects, each reacting to the conflict between TS and SR in different ways. TS and SR disagree about their approaches to professional direction for the group, but through a discussion it was revealed that the anger they display towards each other has its roots in individual experiences. BB and TO also had concerns, and expressed hopes that a change in the relationship between TS and SR would help everyone. Therapist encouraged Clients to learn to defuse contentious moments by trying to identify the true sources of their anger. Clients were able to empathize with each other, and were directed by Therapist to apply this knowledge to future situations in the hopes of decreasing conflict.

Diagnosis:

Z63.8: Other Specified Problems Related to Primary Support Group

Z56.9: Unspecified Problems Related to Employment

8

VITO SPATAFORE

Intake information: Client is a 47 year old man seeking therapy for help with work-related stress. Client works in the construction industry, and describes feelings of frustration with a lack of advancement in his career, despite feeling like he has earned both a promotion and a raise due to his work ethic and dedication to the business. Client is married, with two children, and reports no previous therapy experience.

Vito Spatafore sits on the couch across from me, scanning the newspaper sports page. "This would be my best month ever if it wasn't for the freakin' Jets. Did you see the game?"

"I did," I say. "Crazy ending."

"I know, right? I've been making book half my life, so I know the value of laying off bets, but with all this money coming in on the Jets, and me knowing a guy who knows a guy who knows their trainer, I figure knowing they're not gonna to cover the field the night before has gotta be worth a half a point in that weather. So I keep the action for myself, and of course they lose on a last-second field goal and that half point bites me in the ass."

I nod in sympathy. "Lesson being, never bet on the Jets."

"I never learn." Vito shrugs, and we sit in silence for a moment, as I give him space to bring up a new topic. He doesn't, so I move on.

"Any update on your work situation?"

"Well, I did like you said and had a good talk with my boss. I was clear about the things I've done to deserve a bump, and I made a clear ask for a promotion. I thought I communicated well. I mean, I didn't get the bump right then and there, but I can tell he really thought about it, and I think it's gonna happen for me soon. If there's one thing about me he can be sure about, it's that I'm a good earner."

"Great, I'm glad to hear that. Both the result of your conversation, and how you approached the conversation in the first place."

He nods, then another awkward silence. I sit with it, waiting to see what comes up for Vito, who looks like he's struggling with something. Finally he speaks.

"I'm not sure how to say this..."

I nod, waiting.

"Everything we say here is confidential, right?"

"That's right."

"Good." Another long moment, then: "I think I'm attracted to men."

I'm surprised, but I try not to show it. Instead I nod, resisting the urge to respond, and wait for him to speak at his own pace.

"I mean, I'm not gay," Vito continues after a moment. "I'm married, I got two kids, I love my wife, I love football... But I also happen to find myself attracted to men."

Vito looks at me expectantly, but I don't know what to say yet, so I don't say anything.

"You gonna say anything?" he finally asks.

"Oh, I'm sure I will, but I want to hear more from you first," I say.

Vito sits there, processing his feelings about what he's just said. "This is the first time I've ever said that out loud. It's the first time I've ever actually told anybody. You surprised?"

I think for a moment before responding. "Yes and no. I mean, it's not like I suspected anything about this before now, so in that sense it is a surprise. But it's also the case that, oftentimes in therapy the real issue that a client needs to explore is one that takes time to warm up to revealing."

"That makes sense," Vito agrees. "How long have we been doing this?"

I check my notes. "This is our fourth session. We've talked about work mostly, and while I think that was important to talk about, it makes sense that there might have been something bigger."

"Oh, this is bigger alright." Vito takes a deep breath. "I can't believe I told you. I can't believe I said it out loud."

"How does it feel to say it out loud?"

Vito takes stock of himself, and seems surprised. "It feels good. I feel... lighter."

"I can understand that," I say. "There's something about verbalizing the things that we feel, thoughts that we've had in our heads for a long time, something about saying them out loud can change our perception and understanding of them."

Vito now seems a little more concerned. "The thing is though, I work in a business where being a *finook* is not okay."

Vito then looks at me as if considering a new thought. "You're not... Are you gay? Did I just offend you?"

"I'm heterosexual. And as far as being offended, that's not a word I would use to talk about gay people, but I'm not going to judge you if you use it. That's another issue we can discuss, but right now I'm here to support you as you process all this."

"Thanks. So, being a *finook* is a no-no in my world. I mean the idea of a guy dressing up like a girl, or being all queenie like, singing and dancing, that's unacceptable for a guy in my position. Of course it's not like that for me. I'm a happily married man with two kids and a steady job and a place in the community. I'm just a straight guy who happens to also like men. That doesn't mean I'm gay, does it?"

Vito seems to plead with me to justify his feelings, but I

demure and try to take a more open-ended approach. "I'm not here to tell you what label you should have for yourself. Let's not even worry about how to categorize this, and just focus on your experience. What's it like having this realization about your sexuality in relation to the parts of your life that you say could never accept it?"

"Well, I'm keeping it a secret, that's for damn sure. I'm compartmentalizing, according to an article I read. I've been really, really careful. Madonn', if my boss ever found out? I'd be a dead man. Being gay just isn't acceptable in the construction business. It's not an option. And my family? They'd be gutted. The man who supports the family, who lays down the law, who makes the decisions, going around hooking up with random men? They'd be shocked. Again, not an option."

"Vito, the way you talk about your options, do you feel like you have to pick an option? To actually do something about it, to take action?"

Vito considers this. "I don't know."

"Because I want to point out, the fact that you were brave enough to talk to me about this, that was an action you took. You've just done something. But I was just curious if you felt like you had to continue, to address this is in a more concrete, or formal way."

Vito continues to look conflicted. "I don't know. I don't know what I should do, what I want to do, or if I should do anything at all. Can I keep living this double life like this? I don't know, maybe? But it seems like the best idea right now."

"That's fine, I don't want you to feel like you have to walk out of here today with a plan of action. I hope that just discussing this, exploring it more, will clear things up for you in a way that ends up revealing a course of action to you, if that's the case, without you having to decide on something before you know what really feels right."

Vito nods along as I speak. "Yeah, that sounds good. Sorry

about dragging it out so long. I must have really bored you with all that bookie talk."

"No worries, that's all part of the process. And I love the bookie talk, by the way."

We sit for another quiet moment as Vito thinks. "The double life thing, it hasn't been terrible. But it's starting to get harder. I mean, the more comfortable I get being around men, the harder it is to adjust to coming back to reality."

"How have you been managing this double life?"

"Well, I found some spots for guys like me to meet up. And a few clubs where it's safe to let my hair down. Dress up a little, bust out the leather. I had to put in a lot of legwork to find places that I'm sure nobody I know's going to show up at. So, I guess I'm in a good place. For the moment. But here's what scares me: What if it gets bigger?"

"What if what gets bigger?"

"This *finook* inside me. What if I keep doing this but the gay part grows? If I'm not careful, if I start enjoying it too much, it might become a bigger part me to the point where it gets over half, and if that happens… I mean, will I be officially gay?"

Again I chose to avoid giving Vito a direct answer. "So, letting yourself have these experiences with men fulfills some part of you, and the worry is that if you continue like this you might reach a point where you prefer that life over what you call the "normal" one?"

"Exactly. I think I wanna go with the, what do you call it, the repressed situation. You know, where I have this secret life and nobody ever finds out and I take it to the grave."

"Would that be the easiest path?"

"I think so."

"Why?"

"Because that way, things wouldn't change. I'd keep my job, my family. Blowing all that up, it'd be too much."

"Well, I want to let you know I support you in any decision

you make. And while we explore this part of yourself and talk about it in a supportive way, I don't want you to feel like I'm leading you to make a decision. An issue like this can take time to process, and there might or might not be changes in your life as a result. I'm just glad you've brought it up here. I hope you feel better after talking about it with me."

"I do," says Vito. "It's funny, I always feel better after our sessions, even if nothing's really changed."

"Well, something has changed. You've talked about the issues you're dealing with. It's not just in your head anymore. It's out in the world. Albeit a very small, confidential world."

"Right. This is all complete confidential, right?"

"Completely."

I sit in silence with Vito for another minute, then sneak a look at the clock.

"Well, we're just about out of time for today. Thanks for trusting me with this, Vito. Was it hard to share?"

"Yeah, but also not that bad. I mean, I trust you, and I guess if I'm going to admit to something like this, this is the place to do it."

I get up and open the office door for Vito, who stops and turns to me as he reaches the door.

"I really appreciate your support, Phil. And to show my gratitude, I wanna give you a gift."

"That's very nice of you, but I don't accept gifts from clients, it's an ethical policy."

Vito nods, then leans in towards me. "Take Green Bay and the points." Then he slaps my cheek playfully and leaves.

I close the door behind him, then sit down to write up my notes.

Clinical notes: Client presented with an engaged affect, updating Therapist on work developments. Client then made a major revelation, sharing with Therapist that he is attracted to men, and is reassessing his sexuality, exploring the idea that he might be gay. Client is currently determined to maintain this secret and live a double life, as a heterosexual married father as well as a man attracted to other men. Client feels relatively safe in his separation of these two worlds, emphasizing to Therapist how badly his employer would take this news. Client reported feeling better after having revealed this to Therapist, but is afraid that if he gives this part of his life too much space it might take over and become a larger part of his identity, something Client says he does not want.

Diagnosis:

F43.22: Adjustment Disorder with Anxiety

Z70.9: Counseling Related to Sexual Attitude, Behavior and Orientation, Unspecified

9

AVON BARKSDALE AND STRINGER BELL

Intake Information: Clients are 33 year old men who are business partners, and have reached out for couples therapy to help resolve issues regarding their work, identifying a difference of opinion about the future of their business and what path to take to achieve their long-term goals. Clients have been business partners for approximately fifteen years, and report being best friends going back to childhood. Clients are both single, and indicate no previous therapy experience.

Avon Barksdale and Stringer Bell sit on the couch across from me, Avon in a basketball jersey and sneakers, Stringer dressed more formally in slacks and a sweater.

Avon shakes his head in disbelief. "I can't believe I'm doing this shit," he says. "A brother like me in therapy? Sheeeeit."

"Yeah, it's weird, I gotta agree," replies Stringer, "but Levy was pretty sure it would help."

"I don't wanna hear another word about Levy, I never trusted his ass. He's always got some ulterior motive that's all about himself."

"Maybe, but he's done a lotta good work for us. That's been money well spent."

I speak up and join the conversation.

"So what I'm hearing is that you're a little uncomfortable, or at least unfamiliar, with all this. You said in your intake paperwork that neither of you had ever been in therapy?"

"Hell no," says Avon. "This is some white folk shit."

"Okay. So in the world you're from, people don't go to therapy?"

They look at each other and share a laugh.

"Ain't no therapy in West Baltimore," says Avon. "You just play the game, or you don't."

"Word," agrees Stringer, and they bump fists.

"Well, let me start us off by saying that I work with the full spectrum of people all along the socio-economic spectrum," I say. "Of course, I am a white guy, from a place different than where you're from, but for the purposes of our work together, I want you to know that I'm here to hear and support you, no matter what race, religion, or ethnicity."

"Appreciate that, Phil," says Avon. "That's some real American shit right there."

"I read in your *Psychology Today* profile that you specialize in working with business partners?" asks Stringer.

"That's right, it's a specialty of mine. It started with my work with writing teams, drawing from my experience as a screenwriter and producer. Through that work I started to appreciate that work couples can benefit from couples therapy just as much as romantic couples."

Avon looks skeptical. "I thought couples therapy was just for brothers and they hoes?"

"Well, there's traditional couples therapy for romantic couples to learn to communicate better and resolve their differences with less conflict, but the same interventions can apply to non-romantic work relationships. Romantic couples are often joined by a marriage or by children. Work couples are joined by a business. And similar issues can come up, only work couples don't usually think of therapy as an option in the same way that romantic couples do."

"I ain't been thinking about this as an option at all," says Avon.

"But this here might be just what we need," pitches Stringer. "Someone to help us resolve our differences about the business and shit. You feel me?"

"I'm here, ain't I?"

"Okay, with all that being said, why don't you tell me about your business, and the conflict between you about it."

They look to each other warily.

"Is what we discuss in here privileged information, like with a lawyer?" asks Stringer.

"Everything we talk about here is completely confidential," I answer. "However, there are exceptions for child and elder abuse, mentions of self harm, and I also have a duty to report any threats to identifiable victims."

They both consider this, then have a whispered conversation. After a moment, they turn back to me.

"Okay, see, our business is that we sell ice cream," explains Avon.

"Ice cream, got it," I say as I jot this down in my notes.

Stringer looks concerned. "Are you taking notes on a criminal conspiracy? I mean, on our ice cream business?"

"I take notes with all my clients. I write down names, details, statements, things we can refer back to in future sessions."

"But it's all confidential?"

"Yes, although within the limitations I've already described."

Avon leans forward, rubbing his hands together. "Okay then, here's the thing. We've been in the ice cream business a long time. Me and my boy here. We built it up from nothing, starting from when we were young 'uns all the way till now, as grown ass men. But it's not easy. I mean, it's never been easy, but lately the ice cream game has done changed. And we're not straight on how to deal with those changes."

"We have some disagreements on how to adapt our business

to various changing economic conditions," says Stringer. "I'm trying to make decisions based on information and facts, business principles. But Avon, he's more of a gangster."

"An ice cream gangster," clarifies Avon.

"Right," continues Stringer. "And I'm more of an ice cream businessman. You know, appreciating the economics of the situation."

"You been spending too much time at that white-bread college, boy," Avon says dismissively.

Stringer ignores him and continues.

"Avon was in jail for a while there on charges of distribution of… ice cream, and I've been running things while he was away. During that time we developed a supply chain problem, and the quality of our ice cream went down, causing us to lose customers to our competitors who had higher quality ice cream, even though we had control of the corners. I mean, the ice cream parlors on the corners. So, instead of continuing to sell an inferior product to a decreasing client base, I made the business decision to join forces with our competitors, sharing our desirable ice cream parlor locations with them in exchange for access to their higher quality ice cream. Everybody wins."

"We did not win!" Avon almost jumps out of his seat. "We lost because we look like pussy ass bitches. Giving up even one inch of those corners means—"

"Ice cream parlors," reminds Stringer.

"Stepping back instead of stepping up affects my rep, and I've been building my rep my whole life," Avon continues. "The ice cream business will come and go, but the one thing I'll always have is my name, and ain't no price on that."

"Okay, I think I can see the basis for your disagreement," I say. "Stringer, you value approaching problems from a calculated, business-oriented point of view, while Avon, you appreciate the more emotional aspects of the situation."

"Yo, I'm a Barksdale. That name means something to people."

"Yeah, but the name don't mean shit if the ice cream is weak," counters Stringer. "We're losing street cred because Prop Joe's ice cream is pure. It's coming straight from the Greek. I had to make a move, and you were locked up."

"It don't matter how pure your ice cream is, long as you own the parlors."

I try to move the conversation in a different direction. "Stringer, what was it like for you to be in charge of the business while Avon was in jail?"

"It was tough, man. The quality of the package got bad real fast, and then I gotta hear about customers going over to East Baltimore for that good ice cream. And with Avon in jail, my contact with him was limited. I had to make some decisions on my own."

"That must have been difficult," I say.

Stringer seems to appreciate my empathy. "It really was."

"Avon, can you acknowledge the feelings Stringer is sharing here? How it was hard for him to run the ice cream business on his own while you were in jail?"

"Yeah, I can, but that don't mean he should be cooperating with the enemy, giving up my parlors."

"Okay, I get what you're saying, I see the reasons you feel the way you feel. But I want you to try saying that again, in response to what Stringer just said, without the 'but.'"

Avon looks confused. "What do you mean?"

"I mean, I want you to respond to what Stringer just said again, and stop before you use the word 'but.' I promise, we'll get to your concerns, but first I want to make sure we focus on making space for Stringer's feelings."

Avon looks skeptical. "This is some wack shit."

"Just give it a chance," I encourage him. "Stringer, tell us again what it was like running the ice cream business while Avon was in jail."

"It was hard. Shit went south and I had to clean up the mess by myself."

"Okay, Avon, tell Stringer you heard him."

Avon sighs. "Fine," he says, turning to Stringer. "I hear you, dog. I feel bad I was away and you had to deal with this shit on your own. I know you meant well."

"I appreciate that, dog."

I let them sit with this for a moment, then continue.

"This feels good to me. If you guys can support each other's feelings, validate and accept each other, I think it'll lessen some of the conflict around these business decisions. Okay, now Avon, it's your turn. Tell Stringer how you really feel about his business decision about the ice cream co-op."

"It's fucked up, man. I feel hurt," says Avon. "Like you wounded my pride. I know you be thinking in terms of business school and shit, but I'm straight from the streets, and when I hear you giving up my parlors that I fought and bled for, I go crazy."

"I hear you, brother. And I'm sorry. But I had to do what—"

"No buts," I interrupt.

Stringer shakes his head. "Right. Avon, I hear you. I was right there fighting and bleeding for those parlors with you. I wanna find a way to make it right. For real. I love you dog. We started this together, we gonna finish it together."

Avon considers this for a moment, then agrees. "No doubt."

He reaches out his hand, and they shake, then hug, getting a little emotional.

I push the box of Kleenex towards them, and Avon takes one, dabs at his eyes.

"I can sense the emotions you guys are feeling here. And I want you to remember how it felt to show each other that you're really listening to each other, that you're hearing each other. And when you're in the heat of the next argument about the business, some difficult decision you have to make, and you're driving each other crazy, I want you to remember this feeling you're having right here, and maybe it'll help."

They nod silently. Then Avon's pager beeps, and he checks it.

"It's the Greek. We gotta bounce."

They stand up, and I walk them towards the door. As I open it I see Stringer has detoured towards my chair, and rips the notes out of my notebook and stuffs them in his pocket.

"Sorry, Phil. Strictly business," he says.

Before I can protest Avon pulls out a wad of bills and peels off a couple, stuffs them into my hand.

"For new notepads and shit."

Then they exit. I close the door behind them, and sit down to rewrite my notes.

Clinical Notes: Clients presented with cautious affects, both having never been in therapy before and unsure of how to approach the experience. Clients shared their disagreements about business dealings, with SB advocating for a more traditional business approach, while AB displayed a more emotional reaction to business related events. Therapist worked with Clients to share emotions behind their reasoning more clearly, and to focus on showing that they truly hear each other in a way that might create more empathy and mitigate future conflict.

Diagnosis:

Z63.0: Relationship Distress with Spouse or Partner

Z56.9: Other Problems Related to Employment

10

RACHEL GREEN

Intake Information: Client is a 24 year old female seeking therapy for help processing recent last minute decision to call off wedding, and ensuing conflict with parents, especially father. Client also reports experiencing stress resulting from her historic reliance on parents for financial support, which is in conflict with newfound desire to find her own path in life. Client is single, has no children, and indicates no previous therapy experience.

Rachel Green sits on the couch across from me, full of energy, gesturing and bouncing in her seat as she talks.

"I was sitting in the bridal suite, in my wedding dress, five minutes away from saying 'I do,' and I'm looking around at all the gifts from the registry, a waffle maker, champagne glasses, this silver gravy boat, and suddenly I had this realization that hit me like a bolt of lightning: I don't want to get married! Even though I said I did, and I went along with the wedding plans, and my parents paid for this lavish wedding and friends and family flew in from all over the country. Talk about pressure. But I didn't want to marry Barry! Is that crazy?"

I shake my head in support. "No, I don't think that's crazy at all."

"Thank you! I needed to hear that. Because sometimes I feel like I'm crazy. Plus, I realized that Barry sort of looks like Mr. Potato Head. But another realization that hit me in that moment was how my life was all planned out. I had nothing to worry about. It's like I was on auto-pilot. And suddenly, in one moment, I turned it all upside down. Now I don't know what to do. I don't have a plan anymore. I have no plans!"

Rachel sits back with a loud sigh, contemplating all this. I sit in silence, giving her a chance to continue, which she does.

"This is not how I pictured my life working out. I mean, I'm twenty four years old! I should have things figured out by now, right?"

"I don't know," I answer. "Some people go their whole lives without figuring it out."

Rachel scoffs. "Is that supposed to cheer me up?

I don't address her comment, and instead continue with this train of thought. "The funny thing about life is it often doesn't work out the way we think it will or should. Oftentimes things don't go according to plan. And it's common for people to come to therapy during these life transitions. And getting married, or deciding not to, is one of those transitions."

"So what happens now? How do you help?"

"I'm here to help you navigate this transition. It's in times like this that our lives can feel like a snow globe that's been shaken up, and a flurry of snow has obscured everything. It can feel unsettling, unsure, unsafe. But over time, as we process these events, the snow eventually settles, and we can see the bucolic cabin in the woods with the cute little chimney. We can get a clearer view of our lives on the other side of all these changes."

"Bucolic cabin in the woods," repeats Rachel. "That sounds good. I guess I can see that. And it's not like I'm totally plan-less. I reconnected with my friend Monica, she's going to let me stay at her apartment. And I'll have to get a job." She thinks about this for a moment. "How does one get a job?"

I shrug. "You could get out there and start handing out resumes, or do it online."

"Right, resume, got it." Another moment of her thinking about this, then: "How does one get a resume?"

"Do you have any work experience?"

"No! I've never had a job. I've never needed a job! Nobody ever expected me to get a job."

"What do you do for money?" I ask.

"I have rich parents. Who are slightly less rich now after paying for a cancelled wedding they couldn't get a refund on. My dad has always paid for everything I ever needed. But I suspect that's going to change after this."

"What's your relationship with your dad like?"

The change of topics seems to shift Rachel's mood. "Oh my gosh. Well, it's good, I guess. I mean, I don't hate him. But I'm realizing now that I've never said no to him. I never rebelled. And in exchange for that, he never said no to me. I got everything I wanted. Clothes, a car, college, this wedding… I know he loves me, but I think that's mainly because I've always done everything he thought I should do. I've lived up to his expectations instead of mine. I feel like my whole life he's been telling me 'You're a shoe, you're a shoe,' and I've gone along with it without questioning it, but now I'm like, what if I'm a purse, you know?"

"It sounds like it doesn't matter if you're a shoe or a purse. The point is that you need to find out for yourself just what accessory you are."

"Exactly!"

"Have you told your father this?"

"Are you crazy?" Rachel blurts out. "I had to give him a couple of days off after the wedding to not have a heart attack. Either from the surprise of me calling it off, or the shock of seeing his next credit card statement."

"It's common for clients to come in here and talk about how they struggle to clearly explain their feelings to the people in their lives, in their relationships," I say. "Then we talk about how they feel, and they can usually be pretty clear about things. And what they tell me is often exactly what they need to tell their people. So, maybe you should consider telling your dad what you just told me."

Rachel pouts. "But I'm afraid he'll get angry."

"From what you've told me about him, he probably will. But you can't control that. In fact, much of the conflict in relationships is a result of people not sharing things they're afraid will end up creating conflict. All you can do is be honest about your feelings. How your father reacts is up to him."

"Sure, but he's threatened to cut me off," Rachel says, but she seems to realize something new as she says this. "Which actually might be just what I need. I mean, maybe I need him to cut me off. Maybe that's the kick in the butt I need to get started on my own path in life. Even if I don't know where I'm going."

"Well said. Now, we're just about out of time for today—"

"Oh no!" Rachel says, disappointed. "I didn't even get to this cute boy who Monica hangs out with, Ross. We went to high school together, and it's crazy that the day of my called-off wedding I reconnect with a guy I never paid attention to in high school, but now I think I have feelings for him. He's so cute, in a lost puppy dog kind of way."

"Well, we can pick up with that next week."

I cross over to open the office door for her, and before she exits she turns to me. "Oh listen, I'm worried my dad's going to cut up my credit cards, so can I prepay for some sessions?"

"I don't know," I say, considering this. "How many?"

She thinks for a moment. "Fifty?"

I shake my head, skeptical. "I don't think I can do that. But we can discuss a discounted rate if your financial situation changes."

"Oh that would be great! Thanks so much."

She gives me a quick, surprising hug, then bounds out of my office.

I close the door behind her, then sit down to write up my notes.

Clinical Notes: Client presented with a focused affect, relating recent experience of calling off wedding at the last minute, as well as relationship with father, who is financially supportive but has not encouraged Client to explore what she wants to do in life. Client described feeling like her life was all planned out, and then was suddenly thrown into chaos by decision to call off the wedding, and Client is both scared and excited by the idea of taking more control over her life. Therapist and Client discussed how recent events have thrown life into chaos, and that it will take time for things to settle down and allow her to figure out next steps. Client is motivated to continue therapy.

Diagnosis:

F43.22: Adjustment Disorder with Anxiety

Z60.0: Problems of Adjustment to Life-Cycle Transitions

11

LUKE SKYWALKER

Intake Information: Client is a 22 year old male who seeks therapy to explore relationship with father. Client recently found out father was alive after being told he was dead his entire life. Client described a recent encounter with father that was their first meeting, and which resulted in a confrontation that ended badly, leaving him feeling adrift and confused. Client reports experiencing persistent sadness, diminished appetite, lack of sleep, and social withdrawal. Client is single, has never been married, and reports no previous therapy experience.

Luke Skywalker sits on the couch across from me. He's a young man, handsome, wearing a white and grey tunic, and a black glove on one hand. He seems burdened as he slumps back in his seat.

"Sorry if I'm not exactly the life of the party right now."

"That's okay, I don't expect you to be. People don't come to therapy because they're the life of the party. They usually come because they're sad, or depressed."

"That describes me perfectly," he sighs deeply. "Sad and depressed."

"You mentioned in your intake paperwork that a big part of this sadness and depression is a result of your recent interactions with your father?"

"Yeah. This happened a couple of months ago, but I'm still feeling the aftershocks."

"Tell me about it," I say.

Luke sits up, organizing his thoughts. "Well, it's complicated, but long story short, I thought my whole life that my dad was dead, but recently I found that he's not. He's very much alive, and not only that, he's also a pretty bad guy."

"A bad guy, huh?" I ask. "In what way?"

Luke shakes his head, thinking of how to describe him. "He's just mean, pushy, aggressive. Totally unfriendly. In fact, you could call him evil."

"And what was the context in which you met him?"

"It was a work event. And I knew he was going to be there, but I didn't know he was my dad. It came as a total shock. I'm still not sure if I really believe it."

"What does he do exactly?"

"He's in politics. And it turns out we have very different politics."

"Yes, unfortunately it's quite common for political differences between parents and children to be a major source for conflict."

I pause to see if Luke will speak more about this, but he doesn't, so I continue.

"I want to hear more about this encounter with your dad, but first I wanted to ask about what it was like growing up with your..." I read from the intake paperwork. "Uncle Owen?"

"Yes, Uncle Owen and Aunt Beru. They were great. I knew they weren't my birth parents, and they never tried to be, but they loved me and raised me like I was their own son. I mean, it wasn't all fun and games. Uncle Owen could definitely be a stickler about chores and stuff around the farm."

"So would you say you had a pretty good childhood?" I ask.

"Absolutely. But now that we're talking about it, even back then I felt like there was something bigger out there for me. Like there was some other life I was fated to live. I just never thought this thing with my dad would be a part of it.

Luke shakes his head as he reminisces. "I wish I could go back to those days back on the farm. Everything was so much simpler then. Nothing to worry about but going to Tosche Station to pick up power converters." He stares off, thinking about happier times.

I let this moment breathe for a beat, then continue. "What did your Aunt and Uncle tell you about how your father died?"

"They said he was a navigator on a spice freighter, and that his ship was destroyed in a battle during the Clone Wars. I had no reason not to believe them, but in retrospect, I think maybe deep down I didn't."

"Why do you say that?"

"Well, it all made sense after I finally met my dad, and it turned out he wasn't who my Aunt and Uncle said he was." Luke cocks his head, considering a new thought. "See, even before I met him, when I got closer to him, physically, it's like I could feel his presence. Like there was some kind of force between us. And I recognized that I'd had that feeling before, when I was a kid."

"So what was it like, meeting him for the first time?"

Luke laughs grimly. "It was a shock, to say the least. You don't know about all this, because it all happened in a galaxy far, far away, but he's a pretty divisive figure. Totally the opposite of me and my values. He's just a bad guy."

"Was he bad to you?"

"You mean, like, did he try to hurt me or something?"

"I mean, you've described your father as mean, pushy, aggressive, and evil. But you just met him for the first time. So, did he act that way toward you?"

Luke thinks about this for a moment. "I guess not. It's not like he was a complete asshole or anything. He even seemed sort of emotional, actually. It's hard to see his facial expressions, because he wears a mask for work. But now that I think about it, he didn't come off as this totally evil guy everyone hates. I could almost feel some kind of love from him."

I watch as Luke considers this love from his father. "Feelings of love," I say. "That sounds promising."

"Yeah, but things got heated when he asked me to join him at work. And I got really angry. Like, I was yelling at him, telling him I didn't want to be like him, that I'd never join him."

"And how did he respond to that?"

Luke laughs. "Let's just say he didn't take it well. He got angry. And then things escalated. There was a confrontation, a physical confrontation. A fight." Luke holds up his gloved hand. "He actually cut my hand off. And I bailed right after that."

"So the rest of the world thinks your dad is a bad guy, a villain, and even though you had this violent confrontation, on a certain level he was just a man you'd never met before. Your father."

"Yeah." Luke leans forward, rubbing his head. "This is so crazy! The baddest guy in the universe, the guy all my friends are fighting against, this total villain, turns out to be my father. What a crazy plot twist."

I give Luke a moment to process these feelings in silence, then continue.

"I have to say, one of the things about the parent / child relationship is that, when we are in opposition about longstanding issues, dealing with the kind of things that might lead to conflict or even estrangement, it can be hard to remember that our parents don't always choose to be the way they are. They're just acting as parents in the way they were programmed, often by how they were parented themselves. What do you know about your dad's childhood?"

"Nothing up until about two weeks ago. But after this revelation, my relatives filled me in on some of his backstory. Apparently he never knew his father. His mom raised him. And she died when he was young. And then he was on his own. He met my mom when they were pretty young and had me."

"Any siblings?"

"Not that I know of. After I was born he joined the army, fell in with a bad crowd, and disappeared. That's all I know."

"So, even though we've established your father as this villain, you don't really know him very well, do you?"

"No. And I have to say, I don't think I'll ever really get to know him. I can't imagine us sitting down and hanging out like a regular father and son."

"That makes sense. But at least we can think about what your dad's childhood was like and how that informed who he became."

Luke seems intrigued. "Okay. So, how?"

"Well, you said your father never knew his father. And we don't know how he felt about that. But we might assume that it could have been something he regretted. If we were writing a story about your father as character, we might imagine that because of his lack of a father growing up, he might in turn become a father determined to be a presence in his child's life."

"Sure, only in this case it was the total opposite."

"Right. Instead of changing the experience he had, he replicated it. Why do you think he never reached out to you?"

Luke thinks about this for a moment. "Maybe he was ashamed. Apparently he really changed after I was born. He let his anger get the best of him. That's when he really became a bad guy."

"Right. He became a bad guy. And yet, at the same time, he's always been your father."

"Right. He's my father." Luke starts to tear up, getting emotional, feeling the reality of the situation. "I just wish he could have been around growing up. I wish he hadn't become who he became. I wish the situation we're in now wasn't how it worked out. I wish it was different."

He starts to cry softly now. I reach out to push the box of Kleenex on the coffee table over to him, but he motions towards it and it leaps through the air into his hand. Before I can remark on this—

"Look, I can't complain about my Aunt and Uncle and how they raised me, but I can't help but wonder how things could have been if my dad never left. If he never became the person he became."

"I hear you. You find yourself in a difficult situation. I just hope that trying to understand what made your father into the person he is today you might lessen the anger you have towards him for making the choices he made."

Luke sighs deeply, leans back, closes his eyes. "It's all so depressing."

"I get that. In fact, on your intake form you indicated several factors that would lead me to believe you're experiencing clinical depression."

"I wanted to ask you about that. Isn't there medication for that?"

"There is. I'm not a medical doctor, I can't prescribe medication, but I can refer you to a psychiatrist in case you'd like to talk to someone about that."

"Yeah, maybe. It seems like a good idea, but I don't know if I can motivate to go do that right now."

"No problem, I can send you some referrals and if you do end up feeling like you want to pursue that, you can give them a call."

"And would a pill just make me feel better?"

"Anti-depressants can help people get out from under the weighted blanket of depression, but they're not some magical pill that will fix all your problems. What they can do is relieve some of the burden of the depression so that you're better able to deal with the causes of your depression going forward."

"And in my case, the causes are..."

Luke waits for me to finish his sentence. Instead, I wait for him to finish, and eventually he does. "Well, clearly it's all about my dad."

"Yes, and more specifically it's about how this recent interaction with your dad has made you reconsider things about your life that might lead you to feel unsettled and unmoored."

"Yeah. Well put."

BLEEP BLOOP BLEEP. Electronic noises from outside my office.

"That's my ride, gotta go." Luke stands, wiping the remains of tears from his eyes. "This felt good, though. Can I come back next week?"

I look at my calendar. "Sure, I can see you at same time, 11am on Thursday, May the 4th."

"Great, I'll see you then."

I cross over and open the office door for Luke, revealing a humanoid robot made of shiny bronze metal waiting in the hallway.

"Master Luke? The landspeeder is ready."

"Thanks, Threepio."

Next to the humanoid robot is a smaller robot on wheels. It makes a series of BLEEP BLOOP BLEEPs.

"Shut up R2, I was not crying," says Luke as he crosses past them.

I close the door behind them, then sit down to write up my notes.

Clinical Notes: Client presented with a flat affect, describing and exhibiting symptoms of depression. Client spoke about recent encounter with father, whom he was told was dead and had never met before, and how much of a shock this event was. Client described father as mean, aggressive, and evil, and related confusion about how this new knowledge about his father informed how he thought about his own childhood and upbringing. Client described his depression, leading to a conversation with Therapist about depression symptoms, as well as antidepressant medication. Therapist offered referrals for psychiatric consultation.

Diagnosis:

F32.1: Major Depressive Disorder, Single Episode, Moderate
Z62.820: Parent-Biological Child Conflict

12

DARTH VADER

Intake Information: Client is a 45 year old male seeking therapy to help process long time estrangement from son, along with recent reconnection that resulted in conflict. Client has regrets regarding relationship with son, as well as relationship with wife, who passed away many years ago. Client reports feeling unsettled about approach to career, and how emphasis on this part of his life took away from ability to focus on family in the past, leading to current situation where Client feels his priorities have led him to an unhappy place. Client is single, a widower, has a son, and indicates no previous therapy experience.

Darth Vader sits on the couch across from me, an imposing figure in black full body armor with various digital dials and displays. He wears an imposing helmet and a mask that covers his face, muffling his speech.

"It goes back— h*uuuuh-pahhh* —to when I first— h*uuuuh-pahhh* —Padmé. We— *huuuuh-pahhh—*"

"I'm sorry," I interrupt, "but I'm finding it hard to understand what you're saying."

"Right, sorry. I get that a lot."

Darth Vader pushes a button on his mask, and with a hydraulic hiss it opens, enabling him to remove it, revealing his face, which is pale, hairless, and scarred.

"Please excuse the scars, I had an accident involving a river of lava when I was younger."

"That's quite alright," I say reassuringly. "You were telling me about your wife, Padmé?"

"Right." Darth sighs, and leans back on the couch. "We met when we were very young, and over time we fell in love, but there were always barriers to us being together. Our respective jobs made it very difficult. She was in politics, and I started out in the military before transitioning to work for a large multi-solar system corporation. And I should note that my company is not well liked by the general public. We're sort of public enemy number one, actually. The Evil Empire, people call us. And with Padmé's career in politics, we often found ourselves on the opposite sides of issues. But that's a whole 'nother story, we'll get to that later."

I nod, and repeat what Darth has just shared. "So, you met at a young age, developed a relationship, and your careers involved you being on the opposite sides of certain issues."

"Exactly," he continues. "And I grew to love my job. Except I hit a glass ceiling of sorts. My superiors eventually stopped promoting me, and at a certain point I had to keep my relationship with Padmé a secret from them. That's how strong the conflict of interest was. At the same time, my boss, the Supreme Chancellor, was leading somewhat of a double life himself. Eventually he enlisted me to join him in sort of a shadow company within the organization. So I was under a lot of pressure."

"And what was Padmé doing during this time?" I ask.

"She was concerned about me. I was a maniac, working all the time, it's all I could think about. It got to the point where my wife, this woman I loved, I became like a stranger to her. She would complain about my long hours, and I responded with anger. Always anger."

Darth shakes his head wistfully. "I was so quick to be angry.

And the scary thing is, I liked the anger. It was like I was discovering a dark side of myself. She pleaded with me to quit my job, afraid that it was my work that was turning me into this angry person, but I wasn't hearing it. I'm sorry, I know we're here to talk about my son, so I apologize for the tangent."

I lean forward at the mention of a tangent. "It's fine, and in fact, it's the whole point. To me, therapy is an exploration, it shouldn't have a map. Clients will often start taking about one thing, and then a few minutes later find themselves talking about a completely different thing, and then realize they've gone on a tangent and want to return to the original topic. But I like the tangent. I think that the things we should talk about here aren't always the ones we intend to talk about. So, when a tangent emerges, my instinct is to explore it, because it's often the subject we should be talking about, even if we didn't intend it to be. And that's just a long way of saying, please continue."

"Thanks. Okay, where was I?" I resist the instinct to instruct Darth as to where to pick back up, and wait for him to choose a thread.

"Right, the dreams," he continues. "I began to have dreams that Padmé would die in childbirth. Mind you, I didn't even know she was pregnant at the time. And my boss, the Supreme Chancellor, he started telling me about this new tech the company had developed that could save her if she was in danger. At the same time, Padmé was growing more and more alienated by my behavior, to the point where she told me she couldn't be with me if I continued down this path. And then there was a confrontation, and her old friend Obi-Wan was involved, and we fought, and in the heat of the fight..."

Darth's head droops and he shakes it sadly as he continues. "I struck Padmé. In fact, I thought I killed her. And that's when I ran away. I left to start a new company with my boss, and I put the life I had led previously behind me. And eventually I discovered that not only did Padmé survive, but she was pregnant. And I have a son."

Darth stops and sits back now, processing the feelings coming up after telling his story. I sit with him for a beat, letting things settle before commenting.

"That's a lot," I say.

"I know, it's complicated," Darth agrees. "And now we've finally reached the issue I came here to talk about: my son. You see, I only recently found out about him. And he was told at an early age that I was dead. So, essentially, neither of us knew about the other. And as fate would have it, recently our jobs brought us into conflict. He works at a start up, a small group of rebels who stand for basically the opposite of what my company stands for. We met for the first time recently in a work setting, and while it was a shock for me to finally meet my son, it was even more of a shock for him when I told him that I was his father."

"How did he take it?"

Darth chuckles. "Not good. He was *really* mad. And not just because this was a secret that had been kept from him. I think he was disappointed and angry to find out who I was, and what I did for a living. I think, in his mind, I'm some kind of villain. And of course I let my anger get the best of me, and we fought, and I struck him, and he ran away. And now you're finally caught up."

"Got it," I say as I write this down in my notes. "You mentioned in your intake paperwork that you wanted to work on what you might say to him when you meet again?"

"That's right. I need help convincing him I'm not a bad guy. Sure, I've done some bad things, but I regret them, and I want a another chance to be there for him, as his father."

I nod at this, and give it a moment before continuing. "If Luke was sitting right here on the couch next to you, what would you say to him?"

"What would I say to him? Man, there's so much..." Darth thinks about this for a moment, becoming emotional as he shares his thoughts. "I'd tell him I'm sorry I was such failure as a father. That I didn't know about him, and things would have been different if I had. But that's not an excuse. I let myself be seduced by my career, and I lost track of what was really important in life: family. And I hope he can appreciate that, and we can reconnect, and make up for lost time."

Darth sniffles, tears appearing in the corners of his eyes. I reach out to push the box of Kleenex on the coffee table between us over to him, but he motions towards it and it leaps through the air into his hand.

I ignore this and focus on taking in what Darth has said before sharing my thoughts. "I have to tell you, what you just said, the words you want to say to your son... It's beautiful."

Darth is touched. "You really think?"

"Absolutely. I thought we would spend some time examining how you feel, then formulating a way to express this to your son, and that we might have to dig around a bit to figure it out, but what you've just said, it's clear that you've already given this a lot of thought."

"Thank you. Yeah, I guess I have spent a lot of time thinking about this."

"I would suggest you take a moment to write down what you just said. Not so you can read it to him when you see him next, but so you can be clear that you're saying exactly what you want to say, in a simple, direct way. Although that's a picky note, because the way you just said it was perfect. But I find writing things like this down can bring clarity to the emotions that sometimes make things blurry."

"Yeah, that makes sense," Darth says, contemplating.

I sneak a glance at the clock. "Now, we're just about out of time for today. Do you know when you'll see your son next?"

"I'm not 100% sure, but I suspect his company is planning a

surprise pop-up at a larger event we're hosting. So, I think I'll be running into him then. In fact, I hope I do."

"That's great. Not just the fact that your work might bring you into contact with your son, but that you hope you see him. Hope can be a very powerful thing."

"Yes, I agree. It seems I have a new hope. Thank you for your guidance."

"My pleasure," I say.

Darth puts his helmet back on with a snap and a hydraulic hiss.

I cross over to the office door and open it, revealing two soldiers clad in white armor and masks, standing at attention.

Darth is already up and striding towards the door.

"Contact the Star Destroyer and— *huuuuh-pahhh* —alert them to prepare for my arrival," he says as he exits, his voice sounding much more authoritative now.

He exits, and I close the door behind him, then sit down to write up my notes.

Clinical Notes: Client presented with a pensive affect, having put a good deal of thought into how he wants to communicate feelings to estranged son about their relationship history and current conflict. Session began with a great deal of backstory involving wife and their relationship that informed current relationship with son. Client showed the ability to clearly share the things he wants to tell his son, and Therapist supported Client in this desire. Client observed that he felt hopeful about chance to repair relationship with son.

Diagnosis:

Z62.820: Parent-Biological Child Conflict

Z56.9: Other Problems Related to Employment

13

MICHAEL SCOTT

Intake Information: Client is a 43 year old male who has sought therapy at the urging of partner. Client is an executive at a paper supply distributor, and reports satisfaction with job and coworkers. Client states that he is skeptical of talk therapy, and that he is "just doing this to please his girlfriend." Client's partner is concerned about recent episode at work where Client exhibited suicidal ideation during a morale-boosting exercise. Client is in a relationship, has no children, and reports no previous therapy experience.

Michael Scott sits on the couch across from me, wearing a suit, looking around expectantly.

"Where are the toys?" he asks.

"Toys?"

"Aren't there supposed to be toys? You know, train sets, army men, finger puppets?" Michael looks disappointed.

"I'm sorry, I don't have any toys," I apologize. "It sounds like maybe you had some previous experience with therapy as a child?"

Michael scoffs at this. "No, I think therapy is stupid. But on TV therapy there's always toys the kid is playing with while some bald guy with a beard tries to get them to open up about the crime they witnessed. But that could just be the Law and Order talking. I could run out and pick you up some army men or a

Lego set? I drove past several Targets on the way here. And it's a write off for me. I've got, like, three corporate credit cards."

"That's very generous of you, but I'm going to pass," I say. "Thank you, though."

"Okay, well, once your practice starts making some real money, maybe you can splurge on a toy chest," says Michael, with the air of an expert. "Otherwise, there's nothing to do in here but talk."

"That's true. Playing with toys might distract us from having a conversation."

"That's what she said! My girlfriend, I mean. Always with the talking."

"Right, I saw in your intake paperwork that you're here at the urging of your partner."

"That is absolutely, unequivocally untrue," Michael says. "I'm here at the urging of my girlfriend. Partner makes it sounds like I work at a law firm. Or I'm a cowboy." He adopts a western twang. "Howdy pardner! I'm encouraging you to go to therapy to explore the dark side of your personality and existential semi-suicidal urges. Yee-haw!"

"Some people prefer partner, some prefer girlfriend or boyfriend, husband or wife," I say. "But it sounds like you prefer girlfriend."

"Yep, cuz that's what she is. Also, I have sex with her. All the time. So more than a friend, actually. She's my girl-more-than-a-friend."

"Gotcha," I say, as I jot this down in my notes.

Michael leans over to try to see what I'm writing.

"You're not writing these jokes down, are you? Are you some kind of joke thief?"

"No, I'm just writing down some of the things we say in case we want to look back at them in future sessions. Names, dates, phrases, that kind of thing." I shift in my seat, ready to introduce a new topic. "So tell me, Michael, why does your girlfriend think you should be in therapy?"

Michael stiffens, now more serious. "Well, she says it's because she wants me to be the best version of myself I can be. But I think it's more about her. I mean, I'm a successful corporate executive in charge of a large staff of people who look up to me for leadership. And she... Well, she has a bigger, more important job. But that doesn't mean she can't feel inferior to me. She might be the boss at work, but I'm the boss at home. Well, not in the living room. Or the kitchen. But in the bedroom, I control the remote. Although, she makes me keep my TV in the garage. Which is my domain. But I don't think she thinks this is what I should be talking about here. She's probably thinking about the fake-icide."

"Fake-icide?"

"That's the clinical term for fake suicide," says Michael. "You learned about that in therapy school, right?"

"I don't think that's an official clinical term, but in the context of this conversation, sure, it's a thing. Fake-icide. Tell me about that."

"Well, at my place of business there's a warehouse and an office, and the office workers naturally get depressed because there's no risk of physical injury like in the warehouse. Those guys, the blue collar guys, they're always getting fingers crushed and crates dropped on their heads, and my team of white collar workers is missing out on all that excitement. The threat of a paper cut or stubbing your toe on a ream of double-thick cardstock just isn't the same. The safe, secure world of the office environment is lulling them to sleep and affecting their productivity, and I wanted to inspire them, shake them out of their depression, and what better way to do that than fake my own suicide?"

"How do you get from wanting to inspire the troops to faking suicide?" I ask, trying not to sound skeptical.

Michael thinks for a moment, trying to formulate his logic. "I wanted them to understand that depression is a silent killer, and I thought that seeing me act this out, and then bouncing back from it, would inspire them."

"And how did that go over?"

Michael shakes his head. "Not as good as you might think. Although it definitely shook things up. I could definitely feel a change in tone in the office for days after that."

"So, the fake suicide was an effort to reduce depression in the office," I observe. "Do you feel depressed?"

"That's what she said! My girlfriend, I mean. She asked me the exact same question. And no, I don't. Sure, I have moments where I cry in the shower, or can't get out of bed, but I just push those feelings down into a compact little ball deep in my gut, and then I pop in a K-cup, jump in my Chrysler Sebring Convertible, and cruise on in to work."

I nod and give this a moment to settle. "That sounds like a common reaction to depression. We often want to avoid uncomfortable feelings by pushing them down, by ignoring them. But here, the goal is to engage with those uncomfortable feelings, even if it goes against our instincts. I know it's not fun talking about these subjects, but it's what leads us to seek therapy, and a happier life is usually on the other side of those conversations."

Michael looks annoyed. "Uch, I'd rather play with toys. Do you at least have Uno?"

I stay on track. "I know it's annoying, or scary, but let's focus on this conversation. I need to talk to you about suicide. I want to make sure we understand the difference between suicidal ideation and suicidal intent. Ideation, which is common, is the feeling that you might wake up in the morning and wish you didn't have to deal with life. Or the admission that when you go to bed it would be so much easier if you didn't wake up. It's the feeling that life is hard and it would be easier if you didn't have to deal with it. It's a sign of depression."

"Ding ding ding!" Michael seems engaged now. "I'm with you, go on."

"That's different from suicidal intent, which is when you make actual plans to harm yourself. Like buying a gun, or checking to see if the door to the roof is unlocked so you could jump off if you decided to."

"Yeah, I had to do that for the fake-icide. Check the door to the roof. Turns out there was a fire alarm, but I disabled it," he says. "I guess I should turn it back on eventually."

"So just to clarify, are you currently having thoughts about suicidal intent?"

"You mean, would I really off myself? The answer is no. With this head of hair? No, I've got too much potential."

"Great, I just had to confirm that. How about suicidal ideation?"

"You mean, like, being really, really depressed?" Michael considers this for a moment, warming to the possibility. "Yes, I believe I might have a touch of that."

"Tell me about your experience of depression."

"Okay." Michael starts to talk, but then stops and thinks, and as he thinks he becomes more somber. His eyes tear up, his countenance changes. He opens his mouth to speak, but thinks better of it, struggling to formulate the words.

After a moment of this struggle, he seems to will himself into a different mood, taking on a robot voice. "Depression? Does not compute. Your humanoid clinical terms confuse me, bleep bloop bleep."

I lean back and smile. "You are certainly quick with a joke."

"That's what she said!"

I choose not to respond and instead sit in the silence with Michael, who seems to grow more and more uncomfortable. I can sense his desire to break the silence, which he eventually does.

"What about Connect Four?" Michael asks. "I could probably get that in a package deal with Operation and Sorry."

"You're a funny guy, Michael. I'm a funny guy too. I used to write comedy for television and film. My job was to be funny. And the best comedy, the biggest jokes, came out of tension. Like, when we were writing a scene that was the resolution of an episode, we'd write the serious part first. The stuff about real emotions and conflict between characters. And the more serious the moment, the greater the tension, the funnier the joke would be that relieved that tension. Because we naturally don't want to feel tension. We want to feel that tension broken by a joke. That's what makes for a big laugh."

"That's true. Comedy science, 101."

"Now that I'm a therapist, the tension sets up the joke in the same way. We talk about serious stuff in here. And often times as we're sitting here in silence, feeling the weight of this seriousness, I think of a great joke that would cut the tension. But I don't make that joke. Because the point of what we talk about here is to embrace the reasons for that tension. To talk about them seriously. And if we undercut them with a joke, it makes it easier to avoid them, and then we never actually resolve them."

Michael sits with this for a moment, thinking about this in a serious way. "That makes sense. But it's so not hard not to make a joke!"

"Believe me, I know. But lots of things are hard."

"That's what she said. Hi-yo!"

I sit and wait for the funny moment to pass, letting Michael process what we've just talked about. He thinks for a long moment, then finally speaks.

"I can't not make a joke."

"Why not?"

"It hurts not to. But I guess what really hurts is what I'm avoiding."

"What are you avoiding?"

Michael softens, seeming very vulnerable in this moment. "I just want people to like me. And I'm afraid they don't. My employees, my girlfriend… I'm a likable guy, right?"

"I think you are. But the person whose opinion about that is the most important is you."

Michael looks confused. "So, you think I don't like myself?"

"Many of us have a critical inner voice that believes we're flawed and unredeemable, that we don't deserve the love of the people around us. This inner critic is often not really our own voice, but the internalized voice of someone else who was critical of us in the past, often a parent. We tend to take on this critical thinking about ourselves we learn from others, internalize it, and carry it with us. It can seem like it's our true selves, but I think we're better off externalizing that voice, and working to realize that that's not how we truly see ourselves."

"Yeah, that makes sense. My stepdad wasn't the nicest knife in the drawer."

"Does the critical voice about yourself, your own inner critic, does it sounds like your stepdad?"

"Yeah. Yeah, a lot."

Michael sits for a long moment, deep in thought. After a moment, his hands come together in his lap and he murmurs to himself.

"One two three four, let's have a thumb war."

Michael has a solo thumb war, doing the voices of each thumb as they struggle with each other, until one is the victor. Then he takes a deep breath.

"Well, I feel better. This was great! Is now when you tell me we're just about out of time for today?"

I check the clock. "Actually, we are just about out of time for today."

As I rise to open the office door for him, Michael asks, "Do I have to come back?"

"Would you like to?"

"I don't know. I'd have to bring some toys."

I nod in agreement. "I'd be okay with that."

I open the door, revealing a gangly, bespectacled man in a brown suit who had been listening in.

"I thought that went great, Michael!"

"Shut up, Dwight."

I close the door behind them, then sit down to write up my notes.

Clinical Notes: Client presented with an engaged affect, making many jokes over the course of the session, and focusing on the lack of toys in the office. Client acknowledged girlfriend's efforts to have him engage in therapy, and admitted he was feeling depressed regarding events in the workplace and in his relationship, leading to a team building exercise where Client faked his own suicide. Therapist provided psychoeducation regarding suicidal ideation vs suicidal intent, and confirmed Client has no intention to self-harm. Therapist and Client explored the nature of humor as a defense mechanism, with Client recognizing his tendency to joke about serious subjects as a way to avoid engaging them. Client expressed interest in continuing therapy, but with toys.

Diagnosis:

F43.25: Adjustment Disorder with Mixed Disturbance of Emotions and Conduct

Z56.9: Other Problems Related to Employment

14

FEZ

Intake Information: Client is a 16 year old male seeking therapy for difficulty adjusting to new school and new country. Client is a foreign exchange student living in Wisconsin. Client describes being concerned with wanting people to like him, and anxious about revealing details of his own personality for fear of being rejected, as well as dealing with the stark cultural differences between current social environment and his own country. Client is single, and reports no previous therapy experience.

Fez sits on the couch across from me, dressed in vintage 1970s style clothing, his hands in his lap, posture erect.

"I have never been to therapy before," Fez says. He speaks with a foreign accent, but it's vague enough that I can't quite place where it's from. "We just sit here and talk, yes?"

"That's right," I say. "Think of it as a conversation."

"Okay. This is all so new to me. In my country we don't see therapists, we just whisper our problems into a bottle and throw it into the volcano."

"I see," writing this down in my notes. "Where exactly are you from?"

"Oh, it's small country most people have never heard of. And it's very different from this country, that's for sure. But I love it here. I'm making new friends!"

"That's great. I see that you're a junior in high school?"

"That's correct. I was terrified that I wouldn't make any friends, that people would tease me and throw cucumbers, but it turns out I found some pretty cool kids who have taken me under their wings. I made friends!" Fez exclaims joyfully.

"I'm glad to hear that," I say. "Was that was a pretty big concern for you, making friends?"

"Yes, that was my number one concern. I was bullied horribly at my previous school, teased mercilessly, and I am doing everything in my power not to relive that experience. I am so thankful for my new friend group."

"Tell me about them."

Fez leans in, excited to share. "Well, there's Eric, who is a nice guy but a pushover. Then there's Donna, who Eric is secretly in love with but it's obvious to everyone. Kelso is stunningly handsome but a bit of an airhead. Jackie is stunningly beautiful but a bit of an airhead. And Hyde is the coolest person I've ever met. And they let me hang out with them!"

"And it sounds like this is a much different experience than the one you had at your previous high school?"

"Oh, it's night and day. At school back in my country, the guys bullied me and the girls ignored me. I didn't have any friends to hang out with. I was so jealous of everyone else. But now, it's completely different. What a country. USA!"

"It sounds like things are working out well for you at this new school. But the nature of therapy is that we don't just talk about the good things."

I let this land with Fez, giving him the chance to choose the next topic of conversation, but he instead sits in silence, although it seems like he's thinking about something.

I prod gently. "Is there anything going on in your life that you don't like, or that you're struggling with?"

"Is there anything going on in my life that I'm struggling with..." Fez thinks to himself for a moment. He shakes his head as if contemplating something difficult, then his posture changes as he slumps forward. His shoulders sag, and he leans forward to unburden himself.

"I'm struggling with the fact that it's all a lie." Fez's accent has now changed. It's no longer foreign; he speaks perfect English, with no identifiable accent. "See, I'm not really from a foreign country. I'm from Albuquerque."

I don't know what to say, so I just nod, taking it in.

Fez gauges my reaction. "Are you surprised?"

"I am," I admit. "Tell me more."

"I'm not a foreign exchange student. I'm not foreign at all. I was born in New Mexico, went to high school there, but I was teased so much it became hell. I spilled chocolate milk on my pants the first day of freshman year and from then on I was permanently the kid with chocolate milk on his crotch. Choco-Crotch, they called me. It got so bad that I dropped out in the middle of my junior year."

"And that's when you came up with this plan to create a new identity?"

"Not quite. First I worked for awhile doing construction, and then I worked at some fast food places, then I got into sales, but nothing really worked out. So I joined the Army, did basic training, spent some time in Afghanistan, saw and did some things I'd like to never think about again. After I was discharged I was thinking about going back and getting my GED, and as I was thinking about high school I realized that I totally missed out on the classic high school experience. And one day, when I was thinking about how much I wished I could have had that experience, I was at a liquor store and saw this beer called Milwaukee's Best, and I thought someplace far away, like Wisconsin, would be the perfect place for me to try again. And that's when I came up with this plan to become a fake foreign exchange student." Fez exhales and sits back.

"That's quite a story," I observe. "How does to it feel to share that with me?"

Fez assesses his mood. "It feels good. I've been holding this secret in for a long time."

"So, you haven't shared this with anyone else?"

"No way. It's got to be a secret forever. And keeping the secret, keeping the lie going, it's hard. Sometimes I really feel like Fez. Like, I forget I had any other life at all. And then I remember, and it's a shock. But then I slip back into the lie, and it starts all over again."

I give Fez time to continue, but it seems like he's said enough for the moment. "Do you mind me asking how old you are?" I ask.

"I'm thirty-seven."

"And what's your real name?"

"Lalo Martinez. But please, just call me Fez, I need to keep in practice answering to that name."

"How did you come up with that name, Fez?"

"It's an acronym. Foreign Exchange Student."

"I see. So, what country are you saying you're from?"

"That's the beautiful part of the plan," Fez says proudly. "Instead of telling people I'm from a specific place, which might lead them to ask questions I don't have the answer to, I'm intentionally vague about my home country, so I can come up with whatever details I feel like and nobody will be able to verify if they're true or not. It's crazy, man. Some of the stories I'm telling, they're so ridiculous, like is there really a country where people act like that? Sometimes I try and come up with the most outrageous stuff and see if people will believe it, and they always do."

I sit and take this in for a moment. "Well Fez, this is a very interesting situation you find yourself in."

"I know, right?" Fez agrees. "On the one hand, I'm finally having the high school experience I wanted, that I deserve. I have friends, I'm well liked, nobody's teasing me or calling me Choco-Crotch. On the other hand, it's all built on a lie. Maybe I can keep it up forever, or maybe I'll get busted tomorrow. I know I'm digging myself a hole here, but I don't see any alternative other than to keep on digging. I mean, cool kids are buying me hot dogs! Cute girls love my accent! It's everything I wanted in high school."

Fez feels the positivity about what he's saying, but his expression changes as he makes eye contact with me. "You think I'm a horrible person, don't you?"

"I don't. I just see a person with good intentions struggling with the choices they've made."

Fez nods, appreciating that. "What do you think I should do?"

"Hmm. Well, I'm not going to tell you to stop living this charade immediately, or to just bury your head in the sand and keep it going. I'm sure you've already considered the possible outcomes of your options. I guess what I would say is, at some point in either your continued high school experience, or your real life, you will face a moment of reckoning where you have to confront your original, inner self, the one who's more comfortable hiding behind the character of Fez."

Fez nods as he considers this, so I continue.

"And I hope that, in our work together, we might be able to explore who this person is, who Lalo really is, and accept his fears and insecurities, as well as find value in him, so that we can at some point in our lives allow Lalo to enjoy the same kind of life as Fez does."

"Man, that sounds great. How do I do that?"

"I can't say exactly. I think it would involve examining the childhood experiences that led you to feel the way about yourself that you feel," I say. "And processing the fear of how revealing your true self would be reacted to by the people around you."

"That makes sense, but living the lie is much more fun. For now, anyways."

"Right, for now. But we don't know how long now will last," I point out.

"Yeah. Well, I'm not ready to get off the roller coaster quite yet, but maybe at some point in the future I will be. Maybe after talking about it with you more. I mean, it's unrealistic to think I could keep this up all through high school. But I'm gonna try."

Fez checks his watch, and then gets up. "Sorry, I gotta cut this short. I'm meeting the guys for some afterschool activities. Which means, hanging out in Eric's basement and getting stoned. I just wish their weed was stronger. Anyways, thank you for your time, and I'm looking forward to continuing to explore this next week."

"Me too." I say, as I rise and cross over to open the office door for him.

"Until then…" Fez now re-adopts his high school foreign exchange student persona, including the posture and accent.

"To you I say, good day," he says.

"And to you—"

"I said good day!"

Fez exits, and I close the door behind him, then sit down to write up my notes.

Clinical Notes: Client presented with an upbeat affect, presenting himself as a foreign exchange student adjusting to high school life in America, but soon revealing he is actually a thirty seven year old American who has adopted this persona in order to relive his high school experience in a more positive way. Client describes being bullied in high school and dropping out, and now, years later, seeing an opportunity to have the high school experience he desperately wanted, which includes making friends and being included in social events. Therapist supported Client as he acknowledged the long term futility of this plan, as well as the inevitability of eventually having to confront his real self and address the issues that led him to adopt this new identity.

Diagnosis:

309.24: Adjustment Disorder with Anxiety

Z60.0: Problems of Adjustment to Life-Cycle Transitions

15

JIM HOPPER

Intake Information: Client is a 42 year old man seeking therapy for support regarding his teenage daughter, who he describes as "rebellious" and "out of control." He reports that a recent fight with daughter was particularly traumatic, and seeks support processing this event and figuring out how to proceed. Client is divorced, and reports no previous therapy experience.

Jim Hopper sits on the couch across from me. He's a physically large man wearing a khaki police officer uniform, and holds his trooper hat in his lap, turning it nervously as he speaks.

"I just don't know what to do with her anymore," Jim says, eager to unburden himself. "Sure, things weren't great between us, I can acknowledge that. And yes, it's partly my fault, but this most recent fight, it was scary."

"I can understand that," I nod along in sympathy. "I have a teenage daughter myself. The anger they're capable of showing, it can definitely be scary."

"Yeah, but El, she's..." Jim's brow furrows as he thinks about how to say this. "Let's just say she's different."

"How is she different?"

Jim shifts in his seat, now uncomfortable. "She's not like the other kids. She had a rough childhood. She doesn't really talk much. She's sort of a stranger in the world we're living in. I'm trying to manage it, to help her, to be a father to her, and it's just not working. It's like a round peg in a square hole type situation."

"I see," I say as I jot this down in my notes. "What is El short for?"

"Eleven—" Jim says, but then catches himself. "She's, uh, the eleventh woman in her family to be named Elizabeth. So yeah, El is short for Elizabeth."

"Eleven women in her family named Elizabeth? That's interesting," I remark, sensing that Jim is not being completely truthful, but not wanting to push him on it.

"Yeah, it's a whole thing. She's adopted, I don't want to get into all that," Jim says, dismissing the topic.

"That's fine," I say, and choose to move on to another subject. "Tell me more about what led you and El to have this latest blowout fight."

"Well, to set up the situation a little more, I took her in recently. She's an orphan, I'm a single dad— I mean, a single guy. I used to be dad..."

Jim starts to get emotional. I sit in the silence with him, letting him experience the sadness. When the tears come, I push the box of Kleenex on the coffee table towards him.

"Thanks," Jim sniffles, taking a Kleenex and wiping his eyes. "I was married before I got divorced. Duh, right?" He chuckles to himself. "We had a daughter who passed away when she was seven. Cancer. It really screwed me up. I felt so helpless. I couldn't do anything to save her."

"I'm sorry for your loss. It sounds like you're still experiencing feelings of grief."

"Oh, I am. And I don't know if they'll ever go away."

"I hear that a lot," I say. "Grief is often something that doesn't go away. People can spend their whole lives waiting for it to go away, and it never does. For most people, it's something we carry with us forever, just like we carry the memory of the loved ones who passed."

"Yeah. That's how it feels." Jim sits for a moment, thinking about this.

"And, does that experience inform what you're going through with El?"

Jim's brow furrows as he considers this. "I think so. It's making me feel the same way. Like I want to save her, with every bone in my body. I want to protect her. I really don't want to fail again. I mean, I guess I shouldn't feel so bad about failing with my daughter because you can't just make cancer go away, but with this, with El and her situation, I think I can really do something to help. But I'm terrified I'll fail."

"That makes sense," I say. "You're taking on the role of her father, and you want to protect her from pain, you want to keep her safe. But it sounds like the irony is that this is exactly what she doesn't want. Here you are trying your hardest to protect her, and this person you're trying to protect, she rolls her eyes and dismisses you."

Jim sits up, activated now. "Exactly! It's like, what I'm trying to do for her, what I know is best for her, is the exact opposite of what she wants from me, whatever that is. I'm trying to protect her from the danger out there, but she acts like *I'm* the danger."

"Tell me about this danger out there."

Jim sits back now, a bit more cautious. "Let's just say her past is catching up to her. She's got a dark and dangerous, uh… immigration status. With some shady characters trying to track her down who wouldn't mind seeing bad things happen to her. And until we can figure out what to do about it, she's got to stay hidden. She can't go to school, or hang out with friends at the mall, all the things she wants to do. There are a lot of rules, which we all know teenagers love, right? But it's for her own good."

"Right, it's a 'for her own good' situation," I say. "Which teenagers never seem to agree with. Especially when the rules prevent them from doing the things most teenagers want to do, so now it's up to you to enforce the rules, which she is moved to rebel against with every bone in her body."

"Of course. That's how it works, I make the rules and she breaks them. But it's not just like, finish your homework, or eat your vegetables. This is a special circumstance. She can't go out alone, she's got to keep the curtains drawn, we have to have a secret knock. I keep telling her that soon this will all change. Soon things will calm down and she can spend time with her friends and her so-called boyfriend, and do all the teenager-y things she wants to do. But she just can't hear me on this. For El, soon is not soon enough. It's like when I say "soon," she hears "never."

"And was there a particular event that led up this most recent blowout?" I ask.

"Yeah, she snuck out!" Jim says this as if surprised but also not surprised. "Which is exactly what I told her *not* to do!"

"Where did she go?"

"She went to school to see her friends. And sure, it's not like she did anything that bad. She didn't wreck the car or get caught shoplifting. But just being outside, taking the chance of being seen, that's really dangerous for her. I can't tell you how panicked I was."

"And I'm assuming this panic was something she felt when you confronted her?"

"My panic?" Jim seems confused.

"I mean, I'll assume here, but I want to hear from you, that this panic you felt, which seems to be pretty powerful as we talk about it, came across in the eventual conversation with her as anger."

"Oh, hell yeah!" Jim agrees, glad to be heard. "Damn right I was angry, and I had every right to be. So, as punishment, I took away her TV privileges. Seems like pretty simple parenting 101, actions and consequences, crime and punishment, you know? And that's when she had her tantrum. And it was a big one."

Jim shakes his head in disbelief. "Why can't she see that what I'm doing is for her own good? All I get from her is anger, eye rolling, sneering at me. I feel like a punching bag."

I lean forward when I hear this metaphor. "Right. I hear that a lot from parents. Especially fathers of teenage girls. It can be frustrating to love a person so much, to want the best for them, to want to protect them from pain, and to have them react like you're the problem, you're the cause of all their unhappiness."

"Right? That's it in a nutshell." Jim sighs and sits back, thinking.

I let the moment linger for a bit, then continue. "The idea of being a punching bag has a negative connotation. Like, if you're a punching bag, it means you're weak, you don't stand up for yourself, you're a pushover. But here's the thing: a punching bag is an important training aid. It's something that's supposed to help. I mean, imagine if El was training to be a boxer. A punching bag would be a big part of her training. The punching bag's role would be allow her to practice her punches. It doesn't dodge or bob or weave. It just takes the punishment."

Jim nods. "I can relate to that."

"Right. Now image if the punching bad punched back. If the punches El threw were returned with equal or even great force. She'd probably get sick of it real fast. She might even grow to resent the punching bag. Instead of something that's helping her, she might start to view it as the enemy. See, your version of being the punching bag involves trying to make her understand you're protecting her from the danger out there. But in the process, she's seeing you as the danger."

"So what am I supposed to do? Just let her do whatever she wants and not care if something terrible happens to her?"

"No, what I'm saying is, when she hits you, when she punches you, metaphorically or not, it's going to be natural for you to get angry in return and want to express it. The challenge here is to just take the punches. To let her hit you. To let her know that you can be a safe person for her to be angry at, because unlike other people in her life, you won't punch back. Let her hit you until she tires out. By not fighting back, you deny her the response that would make her angry all over again. It's like you're playing tennis, and every time she hits the ball to you you just let it bounce past you. You don't return her serve. And pretty soon the game becomes pointless, and that's when things change. Now, it might feel like you're giving up, but I think as El grows and matures she'll appreciate that you approached it this way."

Jim sits and process all this. "That's an interesting take. Sort of passive, but I can see how maybe since it's basically the opposite of what I'm doing now, it might help."

"Show her you can make some kind of comprise. Something that's small, that you can live with, but that also shows her you're making a change. It sounds like El feels like you're slamming the door shut on the rest of her life, so show her you can open the door a crack."

"Open the door a crack. I like that."

Just then the lights in my office flicker, which is odd, because that's never happened before. I notice it with curiosity, but Jim reacts with more concern.

"Oh crap, I gotta go! Thanks Phil, this has been really helpful, I'll probably be back next week but I'll have to let you know."

Before I can open the office door for Jim he's already there and rushing out.

I close the door behind him, then sit down to write up my notes.

Clinical Notes: Client presented with a tense affect, feeling strong emotions after a blowout fight with adopted daughter. Client described fight and events that led up to it, which involve him trying to protect her from outside forces that he declined to describe in greater detail, while daughter rebels against this protection. Client and Therapist discussed the struggles of raising a teenage daughter, and Therapist normalized the feelings of frustration Client described feeling. The Punching Bag metaphor was discussed, in an effort to change Client's feelings about the negative aspects of holding space for daughter's anger, and the challenge of not reacting to her anger with anger of his own.

Diagnosis:

Z62.821: Parent-Adopted Child Conflict

16

MICHAEL AND KAY CORLEONE

Intake Information: Clients are a 35 year old male and a 31 year old female who have been married for five years. They have come to therapy to explore issues related to secrecy and trust, which are important issues for K, who has initiated treatment, while M reports resistance to couples therapy. Work/life balance is also a concern, with K reporting that M's work life takes up much of his time and attention, and there is little disclosure on his part, leaving her in the dark with regards to parts of M's life she would like to be privy to. Clients report increasing experiences of conflict, lack of intimacy, and degradation of trust over the past two years.

Michael and Kay Corleone sit on the couch across from me. Kay seems friendly and warm, while Michael has a cold, formal affect.

"It's nice to meet you both in person," I open.

"Likewise," says Kay brightly as Michael nods silently.

I'm about to continue when I turn to the bodyguard standing by my office door, a large, intimidating man in a dark suit.

"I'm sorry, but we're going to need some privacy."

The bodyguard ignores me and looks to Michael, who looks from the bodyguard to Kay. She nods slightly, and Michael turns back to the bodyguard.

"*Aspetta fuori*, Al."

The bodyguard nods and exits.

I turn back to the couple. "Do you always have a bodyguard with you?"

"It's just a formality," says Michael. "We've had some threats in the past, but nothing serious."

"It goes along with his business," says Kay. She says the word 'business' as if it leaves a bad taste in her mouth. Michael glares at her.

"And what is your business, Michael?" I ask.

Michael looks at me for a moment, considering, then: "I import and distribute olive oil."

I wait for Michael to go into more detail, but he doesn't. Kay shifts in her seat and clears her throat uncomfortably.

I take the opportunity to introduce a new subject. "I see from your intake paperwork that you're here to discuss issues related to secrecy and trust in your relationship. Is that accurate?"

Kay leans forward, eager to get started. "Yes. Things have changed so much for us since Michael got more involved in the family business. It's so different than how it used to be with us. I used to feel like we were a team, like we could talk to each other, make decisions together. But that's changed. Now, I just feel left out. My feelings aren't considered. My opinions aren't taken into account. And I'm sick of it."

Kay exhales, having gotten it all off her chest. I give her a moment, then continue.

"And would you say this change in your relationship has made you more unhappy?"

She laughs. "That's an understatement."

"I see. Kay, you articulated your concerns about the relationship clearly and concisely. Can I assume that you've been thinking about this for a while?"

"Oh, yes. It keeps me up at night. I've been after Michael to try couples therapy for months. I'm glad we're finally here."

"So am I," I reply.

Kay sits back, and I turn to Michael. "Michael, when you hear Kay talk about your relationship like this, what comes up for you?"

"What do you mean?" Michael seems defensive right off the bat.

"What does it feel like for you to hear Kay say what she just said?"

Michael pauses, calculating. "I don't have a problem with our marriage."

I wait for him to elaborate, but he doesn't. It's an awkward moment, but I don't break the tension. Kay looks from Michael to me and back, then shakes her head sadly.

"See what I have to put up with? He'll only say the minimum. It's like his goal is to give me as little information as possible. He reacts to every conversation like it's a police interrogation."

"That's not funny," Michael says, a twinge of anger in his voice.

"It wasn't a joke!" Kay turns back to me. "He's been like this ever since he took this work trip to Italy. It was a last minute trip, and he was gone two years. Two years! And when he came back, he was a different person."

"Michael, tell me about this work trip. It sounds like a long one."

Michael shifts in his seat, changing his tone. "There was an unavoidable work situation that I had to take care of, and this entailed me having to take an extended business trip."

"Where to exactly?"

Michael seems reluctant to continue, but Kay gives him a look. "A small town in Sicily where my father grew up. It really was unavoidable. There were events that happened here that threatened the safety of... the olive oil business. I had to go."

I nod. "You know, when you talk about your business, it seems like it's in relation to your family, and vice versa. They seem intertwined."

"They're one and the same," he says, now calmer, without anger. "My business is very important to me, as is my family. After all, it's the family business. But many people depend on me for their well-being, not just my direct family. It's an extended family, made of relatives as well as in-laws, adopted family, close friends, business associates... The people I work with, they are my family."

Kay jumps in. "And all of that sounds great, I'm not complaining about that. I knew what I was getting into marrying an Italian. I mean, who wouldn't want their husband to stress the importance of family? The problem is, it feels like I'm not included. Sure, there's family meaning husband and wife and kids, but there's this whole other family that I'm not privy to. I feel excluded. And I get no sympathy or understanding from him. This is not what I signed up for!"

Kay ends with anger, and I turn to Michael, looking for him to respond, and he does, engaged now, but trying to contain his frustration.

"My work requires discretion. I can't always share the details with my closest business partners, much less my wife. Which is something I made clear when we got married. She knew exactly what she was getting into. There's my family, and there's my business."

"Yes, but you just described how intertwined they are, the family and the business, and here's Kay saying that it's one big combination that she's sick of being excluded from," I observe.

Michael looks frustrated, and glances over to Kay, who seems eager for him to respond. I keep my focus on Michael.

"She is included. In the way that I deem appropriate. But there are are many aspects of things that she cannot be included in. She's just frustrated that she's not included in the way that *she* thinks is appropriate. But ultimately these are my decisions to make."

"Exactly!" Kay says, vindicated.

"You knew what you were getting into when you married me," says Michael without looking at her.

"You told me you were different than your father!" Kay replies, her gaze fixed on him.

They turn away from each other, in an emotional stand off. This moment feels like it's happened many times before. I let them sit in the silence for a beat before continuing.

"It feels like there are secrets in your relationship, and these secrets are creating resentment."

"Are secrets such a terrible thing?" poses Michael. "I don't expect her to tell me every single thing that happens in her life. I'm okay with not knowing plenty of things. There's a place for secrets, right?"

"Yes, secrets can be appropriate. But when they become an issue that creates conflict in the relationship, maybe that's when it's time to rethink our attitude towards those kinds of secrets."

Kay claps her hands in gratitude. "Thank you. I can't tell you how frustrating it is to have him come home from work and give me all these one word answers, like he's some kind of secret agent who can't talk about what he did that day. It makes me feel like I'm a passenger in a car being driven by a mute. I have no idea where we're going, or how long it'll take to get there, and I have no choice in the matter."

They sit in silence for another beat.

"Kay's doing a good job of expressing exactly what she's unhappy about," I observe to Michael.

"Yeah, she's a firecracker alright," he admits. "That's one of the things I loved about her."

Kay recoils. "Loved? Loved?"

Michael realizes he's stepped in it. "Come on, that's not what I meant."

Michael reaches for her hand, but she yanks it away. They sit in silence for a beat, then Kay turns to me, desperate. "What do you think, Phil? Can you fix this?"

I consider the question for a moment while they look on, eager to hear my response.

"There's a dirty little secret when it comes to couples therapy," I say. "It's something most therapists don't talk about. My job isn't to save your relationship. My job is to explore the things about your relationship that you're unhappy with, the issues and concerns that have brought you here today, the things that you'd like to see change, and then discuss how we might seek the kind of change that gets us to a place where can have a happy relationship. Because the goal in any relationship is to be happy. It would be ideal if that happiness was achieved in this relationship, but that's not always the case."

Kay seems surprised. "I don't understand. Are you saying we should get divorced?"

"No. What I'm saying is that, through an exploration of the issues that have led you here, we will hopefully find a way for you to achieve the relationship happiness you seek in this relationship, but there's no guarantee."

"We are *not* getting a divorce," says Michael sternly. "That's just not an option in my family."

"Your family?"

"Our family."

"Look, let's try on focus on doing the things we can do in this relationship to increase intimacy and get you guys feeling more positive about things. Michael, what do you think about trying to be more forthcoming about your work and its impact on your moods?"

"I'm open to that."

"Great. And Kay, how does it feel to hear him say that?"

"I'm skeptical."

"Why is that?"

"Because he's said similar things in the past and, well, here we are."

"Okay. So, what's something that's been an issue in the past that we can discuss now?"

Kay doesn't have to think about this for long. "Well, there's the thing with Connie…"

Michael goes cold. "You know better than to bring that up."

I become curious, and gently press. "What is this issue exactly?"

"There are some things we cannot discuss here," says Michael.

"Okay, but I want to remind you you enjoy complete confidentiality regarding anything we discuss."

"I appreciate that, Phil, but your idea of confidentially might be different than my idea of confidentiality. And it's in your best interests to adhere to mine."

"I can appreciate that. You can reveal as much or as little about this as you're comfortable with here."

"Michael…" says Kay, pleading.

"I told you not to ask me about my business," Michael replies without looking at her.

Kay turns to me, at wit's end. "You see? He's stonewalling me. This is our problem in a nutshell."

I lean in towards Michael. "Michael, I know you don't want to talk about this. You've been very clear about that. But I think this moment is a chance to show Kay you're willing to at least attempt to make the kind of changes she's asking for. What if you let her ask you about your business in the safety of this room. Just this one time."

Michael considers this seriously, then turns to Kay.

"Fine. This one time you can ask me about my business."

Kay waits for a moment, then asks: "Is it true?"

A long, tense moment, then Michael replies.

"No."

Kay exhales like a weight has been lifted off her shoulders.

She starts to cry. Michael puts his arm around her, comforting her. I give them a moment.

Kay sits up and composes herself. I pause before continuing. "How does it feel to have your question answered, Kay? To have Michael let you in little bit?"

"It feels good. I feel closer to him now."

"Michael, do you see how powerful it can be to share with Kay in this way? How it makes her feel closer to you?"

"I do." He nods, and seems to have taken this moment to heart.

"Good. This moment is important. It's small, but I think it's a sign on the road pointing in a direction that leads towards a happier, more intimate relationship."

A quick knock on the door, and it opens to reveal the bodyguard.

"Roth's plane just landed, boss."

"Right," says Michael, getting up. "Sorry to cut this short."

Kay still sits on the couch, looking disappointed. "What's this?"

"It's the Cuba thing."

"Oh, for Pete's sake..."

"If you want to stay I can have Rocco bring you home."

"I'm not married to Rocco!"

A tense moment, then Kay stands up.

"I'm sorry Phil, but I'm very grateful. I think this has really helped."

"I'm glad to hear that. Are we on for next week?"

Michael is already at the door.

"We'll have to let you know. There are some work developments that I can't—"

"That you can't talk about, yeah, we know," interrupts Kay, as she walks past Michael and out of my office.

Michael takes a white box out of the bodyguard's hands, then turns and offers it to me.

"What's this?" I ask, judging the heft of the box.

"Cannoli. An Italian delicacy."

"Oh, that's okay, I don't need any more dessert."

Michael fixes his steely glare on me.

"Take the cannoli."

I reconsider and accept the box. "Thank you."

The bodyguard holds the door open for Michael and they exit.

I put the box on my desk, then sit down to write up my notes.

Clinical Notes: Clients presented with tense affects, reflecting the tension in their relationship. K is the driving force behind desire for therapy, expressing frustration with lack of intimacy and M's tendency to keep secrets from her. M seems focused on work, which involves his family to a great degree, and is resistant to the kind of change K seeks. Clients were antagonistic during session, with M resistant to sharing his thoughts while K seemed to appreciate having a venue to share hers. Towards end of session Clients were able to interact with more vulnerability, as M was able to share some information regarding work that K appreciated. Continuation of treatment is undetermined, with K desiring to continue but M prioritizing work over therapy.

Diagnosis:

Z63.0: Relationship Distress with Spouse or Partner

Z56.9: Other Problems Related to Employment

17

MICHAEL CORLEONE II

Intake Information: Client is a 40 year old male seeking therapy for support with repercussions of difficult business decisions, as he has recently taken over control of the family business and is trying to move it in a different direction. Client also reports family conflict, both with his ex-wife and direct relatives, mostly in combination with problems related to business dealings. Client is recently divorced, and has previous therapy experience in couples therapy with Therapist, who will now be seeing him individually.

Michael sits on the couch across from me, dressed in an expensive suit, overcoat thrown over the back of the couch next to him. He seems pensive as he tells me about what has brought him back to therapy.

"Events have taken place recently that weigh heavily on me," says Michael, his tone measured. "You were helpful years ago when Kay and I saw you. I know we didn't keep up with therapy after that. I didn't think we needed it. Maybe we did, who knows. But now, with the things that have happened lately, the issues that have come up, the actions I had to take..." Here Michael shakes his head, conflicted. "I find myself needing the kind of counsel that can't be provided by a priest, or a consigliere."

Michael finishes and looks at me with the same coldness and self-control as before, but I detect a hint of a new vulnerability.

I smile warmly. "Well, I'm glad you reached out. It's common for people to experience difficulty and struggles at various points in their lives, and therapy can be a good way to get the extra support we might need to help us through those times. That time in your marriage was one of those times, and now seems to be another one.

"Yes, that's exactly what I was thinking. I'm hoping you can help me."

"So am I. Tell me about these recent events you're struggling with."

Michael sighs and sinks deeper into the couch, as if taking on some invisible weight.

"There have been big changes in the family business lately. My father passed away since we last met, and there was a period of transition, a great deal of uncertainty, and plans were made and changed and made again. I'm taking the lead now, and for the most part, things have worked out as I'd hoped they would. We've successfully transitioned the business from the East Coast to Nevada, setting us up well for growth and prosperity in the future. And I was able to extricate ourselves from a major foreign investment that ended up going badly for those still involved. And perhaps most importantly, a legal matter that had been hanging over our heads for years was finally resolved in our favor."

"I see. It sounds like all the business decisions you describe struggling with worked out well for you."

"They did. But they came at a cost," says Michael. "I had to let some people go. People who worked for us, but were also like family. And some who were actual family. Valuable partners who, for one reason or another, could not be included in our plans for the future. There were difficult decisions I had to make, involving trust issues. Very difficult decisions."

Michael thinks about this, and I pause for a moment before continuing. "I remember you telling me before about the blurred lines between your family and your business. Is this a factor as well?

"Absolutely. I used to struggle with wanting to be involved or not. This is when I was younger. And it was a struggle, believe me. I rebelled against my family, I wanted to do the opposite of what my father wanted me to do. But in the end it seemed like fate made my choice for me, that I would be the one to take over the business, and years later here I am, having achieved the goals I set for us, goals nobody thought possible to achieve. And yet I feel empty inside. I should feel satisfaction, or pride, but I feel nothing."

"Nothing," I repeat.

Michael considers this word differently as he hears me repeat it. "Well, not exactly nothing. There is something. It's like... disgust. I'm disgusted with myself."

I wait for a moment, giving him a chance to continue, but he doesn't.

"I see from your most recent intake paperwork that you and Kay are no longer together?"

"No, we got divorced. Which still feels so odd to say. Nobody in my family ever got divorced. Nobody. They'd rather kill one another than do that. But things got really bad with Kay. After we saw you years ago we tried to put the fighting behind us, started a family, bought a house, all that good stuff. We have two wonderful children, Anthony and Mary. But the breaking point was when Kay got pregnant for the third time. She ended up having a miscarriage. But later on she revealed that she had actually gotten an abortion. Which she did to hurt me. She knew I wanted another son, and she told me this would have been a son. She was mean and spiteful in the sharing of this news with me. And that was the last straw. So, we got divorced."

"I see," I say, staying with the topic, not wanting to direct the conversation.

Michael continues. "The irony is, I thought I was doing all

this work to make the business a success for my family's benefit, but it turns out it made my family life a failure."

"I would push back on using that word, failure. Not all marriages last forever. People get married and divorced all the time, and even if it's a rarity in your family and culture, I would hate for you to think of the experience as a failure."

Michael nods at this. "Thank you. I need to keep that in mind. At work I project confidence. I can't afford to show any weakness. But sometimes, I feel weak inside."

Michael seems on the verge of saying more, but sits here thinking, focused. I wait with him.

After a minute, Michael clears his throat, becoming emotional. "I had to let my brother go."

I wait a beat before asking: "Was that difficult?"

Michael laughs as if it's all he can do to keep from crying. "Was it difficult? It was one of the hardest things I've ever done. But it had to be done. I loved him, of course, but he did things to betray the family. To undermine the business. He left me no choice. I had to have him... I had to let him go."

Michael starts to sniffle, his eyes tearing up. Then he starts to cry. Slowly at first, the tears flowing freely. Then he begins to sob heavily, his shoulders shaking, his body taking on the physical manifestation of his sorrow.

I push the box of tissues on the coffee table towards him, but he ignores it. Instead, his crying gets louder and more intense.

I sit and wait, but I'm startled when Michael suddenly bangs his fist on the coffee table, his grief mixed with anger now. "Why, Fredo? Why?"

A knock at the door, and a voice from outside. "You okay, boss?"

"*Si, tutto bene*!" yells Michael, composing himself. He pulls out a handkerchief to wipe his eyes.

I continue to wait, not wanting to rush him back into the

conversation. Michael takes a few deep breath before addressing me.

"Thank you."

"For what?"

"For letting me cry. I feel better."

"I'm glad. It sounds like you had a lot of grief inside you that needed to be let out."

"Definitely. I don't think I could have done that anywhere else in my life. I guess that's why people see therapists?"

"That's part of it," I agree. "Now, there's most likely still more grief inside you, but I'm glad letting some of it out helped. You thanked me, which I appreciate, but I want to point out I didn't really do anything except provide you with a safe place to express these strong emotions."

Michael nods. "I appreciate that. You've done me a valuable favor, and if there's ever anything I can help you with, any way I can repay you, I hope you'll let me know."

"Who knows?" I say. "Someday, and that day might never come, I might ask you for that favor."

A knock at the door, and it opens, revealing Michael's bodyguard. "Boss, we got that meeting with Tom."

"That's fine, we're done here." Michael stands up to leave. "I appreciate your time and support. Perhaps I'll find myself back here in the future."

"I'm here if you need me."

I rise to walk Michael out, and as he goes he motions to the bodyguard, who carries a white box. "Take my coat. Leave the cannoli."

"Oh, that's not necessary," I say, but Michael ignores me as the bodyguard places the white box on my desk, picks up Michael's coat, and follows Michael out of the room.

I close the door behind them, then sit down to write up my notes.

. . .

Clinical Notes: Client presented with a flat affect, showing little emotion at first as he recounted the business and family developments that led him to seek therapy again, this time individually. Client described work conflict that he was able to resolve successfully, though not without difficulties, as well as his recent divorce and the events that led up to that. Client then reported having to let his brother go from the family business, leading to an extended crying jag in which Client released strong and repressed grief in a carthartic way. Client reported feeling better after this moment, and expressed appreciation for Therapist's support.

Diagnosis:

F32.1: Moderate Major Depressive Disorder, Single Episode, Mild

Z63.5: Disruption of Family by Separation and Divorce

18

MICHAEL CORLEONE III

Intake Information: Client is a 59 year old man who reports struggling with resolving issues related to his family business, and difficulty making the transition into retirement. Client also describes conflict with his nephew and daughter regarding matters both business and personal. Client is single, divorced, with two grown children, and has had previous therapy experience with Therapist.

Michael sits on the couch across from me, his hair grey, his face showing the wrinkles of age, reading glasses hanging on a chain around his neck over a comfortable looking sweater as he updates me on his life since we last spoke.

"Here's another thing that's new with me, Phil: I got diabetes. Look!"

He holds out his hand, which shakes with tremors.

"Does diabetes cause tremors?" I ask.

"It's not just the diabetes. It's also stress," says Michael. "The older I get, the more difficult business decisions weigh on me. I suppose my resolve was stronger when I was younger. Or maybe I was just ignorant, naive. I find myself dreaming of being done with it all, done with the business, just relaxing somewhere in Sicily, getting older in a more peaceful way, not having to deal with the family business anymore."

"Yes, family and business. They seem to have always been intertwined for you, Michael."

"Indeed."

"So, what are the latest developments on the business front?"

"Well, I continue the seemingly never-ending campaign to legitimize the business. When we last spoke I had just moved our headquarters to Nevada, which was a great success. And yes, much of the business is legal now, but I was forced to take on certain investors and participate in various alternative market segments that, if not exactly illegal, certainly exhibit shades of illegality. And my goal has always been to create a lasting, completely legal legacy of a business that can live on after I'm gone."

"Are we still talking about the olive oil business?" I ask.

"Of course," replies Michael, with a mischievous twinkle in his eye. "I found a business opportunity to take the path towards complete and total legitimacy. The thing is, my former partners wanted in on the deal. And if I allowed them to participate, it would cloud the legitimacy, the legality that I sought. So, I had to exclude them. And they did not take it well. These people are not used to being told no. And it became dangerous."

"Dangerous?" I repeat.

Michael sighs sadly and shakes his head. "These people, I worked with them for so many years, provided such wealth to them, yet all my life I've been trying to get away from them. And then I have the chance to finally do it, but they find a way to prevent it."

"So, just when you thought you were out, they pulled you back in?"

"Exactly!"

I nod as I jot this down in my notes. "You also mentioned an issue involving your nephew?"

"Right, Vincent. He's my brother Sonny's boy, he's a lot like his dad. Hot-headed, quick temper, lets his anger guide him too easily. Completely different from my son, Anthony. Anthony's got the soul of an artist, and he's quite literally an artist. An opera singer. I'm actually going to see him perform tonight, the whole family is. *Cavalleria Rusticana,* by Pietro Mascagni."

"Sounds exciting," I offer.

Michael grins and shakes his head, as if appreciating an inside joke. "It's funny, I always thought I would want my son to be my successor. The irony is that, even though I took over the family business, my father never wanted that for me. Yet, here I am. And Anthony, my son, the artist, he's a lot like I was back in my youth. I wanted to break free of the family, to blaze my own way, but circumstances didn't allow it. Fate made a different choice for me. Now my son has the chance I never had. To not follow in my footsteps. And he's taken it."

I sit and look on as Michael considers what he's just said. Then I ask: "Are you jealous?"

"Am I jealous? Of Anthony?" He's skeptical for a moment, but then considers it. "Maybe I am jealous. Yes, I think I am. But I can't change how I've lived my life. The least I can do for my son is give him the change to live the life he wants to live. But there's less pressure on him because, honestly, he's not cut out to lead the family. Which brings us back to my nephew, Vincent. I've decided he's going to be my successor. He might be hot tempered and quick to anger now, but he's shown the ability to control it, and I think as time goes by and his responsibility grows he'll make a fine Don."

"Don?" I ask.

Michael senses my curiosity. "Of the olive oil importing business," he continues. "The only catch is, he's become romantically involved with my daughter, Mary."

"And that's a bad thing?"

"Yes. Because the things that make Vincent right for the job of leading the family business make him wrong as a husband to my daughter. He has the ability to be cold-blooded, he can be ruthless when the situation warrants it. And I don't want my daughter with a man like that. I don't think any father would. So, a condition of promoting Vincent along this path is that he must break it off with Mary."

"And he's okay with this?"

"It was difficult for him, but he made the right choice. Which is also how I knew he was right for the job."

"And what does Mary think about this?"

Michael laughs wistfully. "She doesn't know! Oh, she's going to hate me when she finds out I was behind it. Funny thing about our children. They often want the opposite of what we want for them."

"I'm glad you can appreciate the irony," I say.

"Phil, it seems like my whole life has just been one big irony." Michael chuckles to himself as I give him space to continue. He doesn't, so I do.

"How do you think Mary will react to finding out you were behind the break-up?"

Michael sighs, concerned. "Well, hopefully she won't find out. But that's unrealistic. So, more realistically, I hope it will be a long time before she finds out. Of course, that will depend on how Vincent handles the situation. But if there's one thing I've learned about myself, it's that I'm good at living with secrets. And yes, eventually Mary will find out, and she'll probably hate me for it. But also, eventually, she'll meet a nice man, a professional, a doctor or a lawyer, and she'll find happiness and start a family, and then she'll come around. I'm sure our relationship will get much better in the future, after we put all this business behind us."

"It seems to me like you've become more positive since we last spoke."

"I really have," Michael agrees. "At this point in my life, I have to be more positive, I guess. I have to hope things work out for the best. And right now it looks like they just might."

A knock at the office door, and it opens to reveal Michael's bodyguard, older and more grey-haired himself.

"We gotta leave now to make it to the airport, boss."

"Do you have my suit?"

"It's in the car."

"Good, good." Michael talks as he slowly rises from the couch. "Can't wear a cardigan to the opera, you know."

"Have a great time."

"Thanks, I'm very much looking forward to it."

Michael takes my hand in his, looks me in the eye and gets serious.

"Thank you. For all your support over the years."

"It's been my pleasure."

"But there's something I have to apologize for."

Michael keeps my hand in his, pulling me closer now, getting more serious.

"I forgot the cannoli."

We share a laugh as the tension breaks.

"That's fine, I don't need the extra calories," I say.

"Neither do I!"

Michael crosses to the door, but just before he leaves he turns back to me.

"Do you ever do therapy with fathers and daughters?"

"I do. If you're interested in that, just let me know, and we can find a time to meet."

"Maybe I will."

Then he turns and leaves.

I close the door behind him, then sit down to write up my notes.

Clinical Notes: Client presented with a friendly affect, reflecting on the years that have passed since last session with Therapist. Client updated Therapist on recent business dealings, as well as plans to name nephew as his successor, even though part of this plan involves requiring him to break up with Client's daughter. Client anticipates daughter being upset about this, but hopes over time she will come to understand that he made this decision with her best interests in mind. Client also expressed interest in a therapy session with daughter, and intends to contact Therapist if that is something he decides to pursue.

Diagnosis:

F54.0: Psychological Factors Affecting Medical Conditions
Z62.820: Parent-Biological Child Conflict

19

CARMEN BERZATTO

Intake Information: Client is a 25 year old male seeking therapy to address what he describes as intense anxiety related to his work. Client is a chef who is opening up a new restaurant, a process he describes as overwhelming and all consuming. Client describes physical symptoms such as shortness of breath, loss of focus, and difficulty sleeping. Client describes this anxiety as being the result of opening restaurant, but also acknowledges that it has always been a factor in his life, for various reasons. Client is single, and has no previous therapy experience.

Carmen Berzatto sits on the couch across from me, wearing a plain white T-shirt and jeans. He radiates intense energy as he tells me about the various tasks he has on his mental to-do list.

"I have to get the compressor on the walk-in fixed, I'll probably have to replace the dishwasher, I gotta negotiate some kind of deal with the meat guy to keep the deliveries coming, even though I can't pay for the ones that already have, and that's on top of all the regular clean and prep work."

Carmen takes a deep breath, inhaling through his nose, exhaling through his mouth.

"Good, deep breaths, that should help." I sit with Carmen as he takes a few more deep breaths, then continue. "It makes sense that you're here to talk about your anxiety. I have to admit, I'm getting a little anxious just hearing you talk about all the things you have to do."

"Yeah, I've been told I have that effect on people," Carmen replies. "My anxiety's contagious. I've got enough anxiety for everyone at the party."

"What happens if one of those things on your to-do list don't get done?"

"Oh, everything will get done. If I have to work twenty four-seven, eight days a week, the work will get done. 'The pursuit of perfection is a never-ending road.' That's what a chef I worked for used to say."

"You sound determined," I observe.

"Good. I thought you were going to say crazy."

"No no, that's not a word I would use. There are no crazy people. But there are people so overwhelmed by the stresses of life that their anxiety starts to manifest in physical form."

Carmen grins. "Right, so I'm crazy."

I continue. "This anxiety, this drive for perfection, this whatever it takes attitude, it sounds like something you struggle with, but at the same time it also seems like it's the quality that's enabled you to achieve the professional goals you've set for yourself. Is that accurate?"

Carmen considers this. "Yeah. I mean, all the successful chefs I know are control freaks who work non-stop."

"And yet, those same qualities that enable chefs like you to succeed might also affect your personal life in a negative way?"

He nods. "I'd say that's accurate too."

"That makes sense. It's common for people who achieve great things in their professional lives to have a super power, in your case this drive to achieve, this quest for perfection, yet that same superpower can become a burden when it comes to their personal lives. It's something I see in many of my high achieving clients."

Carmen looks at me, touched. "Aw, you think I'm high achieving?"

"Well, you certainly have admirable aspirations, and the work ethic to achieve them."

Carmen takes another deep breath, and puts his hand on his chest.

"Lately I've been feeling it right here. All the stress. I can't catch my breath. My jaw gets super tight. I start to hear this humming sound in my head. It's like, I don't always notice it, but once I do it's unavoidable."

"That's a classic description of the physical manifestation of anxiety," I say. "In fact, there's a whole school of therapy based on that approach, called Somatic Experiencing, exploring how stress, trauma, and anxiety are experienced physically. You might feel like there's a ball of tightness in your chest, or nausea in your stomach, trembling or weakness in your hands and limbs, or a tingling, pins and needles feeling in your feet and legs."

Carmen looks more interested now. "I'm checking all the boxes, Doc. How do I fix it?"

"There are some interventions I can share with you, but first I want to hear more about the source of all this, the restaurant."

"Sure. What do you want to know?"

"Well, how did you decide that opening this restaurant was something you wanted to do?"

He chuckles to himself, then leans back as he begins to talk. "It's called "The Original Beef of Chicagoland." My dad opened it in '79. He only served one thing: Chicago-style Italian beef sandwiches. Lean cut top round, slow roasted with Italian spices, sliced paper thin, served on a French roll and soaked in gravy. You ever had one?"

"I think so. It's like a French dip, right?"

Carmen looks offended. "I'm gonna pretend I didn't hear that. French dip is the inferior cousin to Italian beef. And it was my dad's thing. He had a passion for the restaurant, but he was a terrible businessman. He ran the place into the ground. Took on too much debt, didn't spend money where it was needed, he just wasn't the guy to run a restaurant. So he bailed. On the restaurant, and on the family. Left my Uncle Jimmy holding the bag. And the rest of us too, I guess. But the one who jumped in to try and save the day was my brother Mikey."

Carmen chuckles to himself thinking about this, then gets sentimental. "Mikey was my hero." He thinks a moment longer, now getting darker. "He killed himself."

I sit in silence with Carmen as he thinks about this. After another moment I say, "I'm sorry to hear that."

Carmen tries to shake himself out of his dark mood. "Thanks. Yeah, it's okay. So after that happened, I took over. I was already on the chef path on my own. The fine dining route. Trained in Paris, worked at the French Laundry, staged at Noma, Chef de Cuisine at a three star in New York. But when Mikey died, I knew this is what I had to do. Come home. Take over the family business. Italian beef. Only I'm going to make this place more than just a beef stand. I want to elevate it. Which is definitely turning out to be a challenge, working with people who aren't used to the high expectations I have for myself, and the people around me."

"Were you close to your brother?"

Carmen seems surprised to be returning to this topic.

"Were we close? Yeah, I'd say so. He was my hero. He was everybody's best friend. Life of the party. But he had a dark side."

Carmen starts to tear up as he talks more about Mikey.

"He had a drug problem. I never knew about it. At least, I don't think I did. I guess I was ignoring it subconsciously or something. But I should have known. I mean, I should have been more aware. Maybe I could have done something to help. He stopped returning my texts, stopped returning my calls. He was making bad decisions with the restaurant, taking out loans, not putting the money back into the business. Just like my dad, actually." He chuckles wistfully.

"Carmen, do you feel like you've had the chance to grieve your brother's death?"

"Sure." But he doesn't seem so sure as he says this.

I wait for a moment before responding. "I hear you saying 'sure,' but something about the way you say it makes me not so sure."

Carmen sighs deeply. "Yeah, I don't know." He shakes his head, tearing up again. "I could have tried harder, you know? I could have done more. I could have confronted him. Made him talk to me. Maybe I could have helped him change. Maybe he'd still be alive. But eventually I got over it. Gotta move on with life, you know?"

I pause to let Carmen think about what he's just said, then continue. "Grief for a loved one's death can be something we think we're done with, but it often has more control over us than we think, and can last longer than we'd like. It's often the case that the grief decides when it's done with us, not the other way around."

Carmen nods as he consider this. "Yeah, that makes sense."

"You used the word 'control' earlier. And the way you talk about the restaurant, you have so many things you're trying to control, so many that it can feel impossible. And people who lose loved ones to suicide, it's common for them, for their grief to be almost compounded, because this thing happened that was out of their control. And they feel bad they weren't able to change what happened, to control the situation. So they search for control in other aspects of their life to make up for it. Do you identify with those feelings at all?"

"Oh, for sure," Carmen says, laughing. "I mean, being a chef is all about being in control. Of the kitchen, of the staff, of every ingredient in every dish that goes out on every plate. I'm an absolute control freak."

"Then it makes sense that you pursue this control over your environment with the restaurant, the to-do list, all those things, especially in light of what happened with your brother, which was so important yet ultimately out of your control."

Carmen doesn't respond to this. He just sits there, thinking. After a minute: "Do you know anything about Al-Anon?"

"Sure. Simply put, it's like AA meetings, but for the family members of people dealing with addiction issues. Parents, partners, siblings."

"My sister's been trying to get me to go to one."

"I think that's something worth exploring. I can send you a list of meetings if you want."

"Yeah, I don't know if I want to do that."

"Why not?"

He shrugs. "I don't know."

I sit for a moment in the silence with him, waiting to see if he'll continue but he doesn't.

"Do you mind if I make a guess about why you don't want to go?" I ask.

"Go ahead."

"If you went to an Al-Anon meeting, you'd be re-opening up the wound of your brother's death, and you'd be putting yourself in a position to feel some pretty intense, and not pleasant, emotions that up until now you've been trying to avoid."

Carmen grins forlornly. "That's it in a nutshell."

"That's totally normal. I will say, though, that while it's normal to want to avoid those feelings, I think that the things you want to accomplish in life, the restaurant, coming to terms with your brother's death, a life with less of this debilitating anxiety and stress, all of that is on the other side of these feelings that you understandably want to avoid. And if you never confront those feelings, or at least let yourself experience them, you'll be putting off the future that's on the other side of it all. So yes, maybe going to an Al-Anon meeting would help."

Carmen takes all this in, nodding to himself. "Can you send me that list?"

"Sure," I say, writing down a note for myself.

"Great. Just what I need, another item to add to the to do list."

"I think you can put this on a separate list."

"Yeah, good idea."

I close my notebook and sit up. "Well, we're just about out of time for today, but I'm looking forward to picking back up with this next week."

"I can't say the same, but I think it's what I need."

I walk Carmen towards the office door and open it for him.

"You should come by when we open and have a beef," he says. "You'll never go back to French dip."

I smile and say, "I'll definitely take you up on that."

Carmen exits, and I close the door behind him, then sit down to write up my notes.

Clinical Notes: Client presented with a stressful affect, showing physical signs of anxiety while discussing his internal experience of it. Client described his work as a chef, along with the stress and anxiety he experiences dealing with multiple day to day problems and issues that are all his responsibility. Client also reflected on the origins of the restaurant he is opening, the suicide of his brother, its effect on him, and the struggle for control over his work environment, especially in relation to how his brother's death was out of his control. Therapist supplied Client with Al-Anon meeting information.

Diagnosis:

F41.1: Generalized Anxiety Disorder, Moderate

Z63.4: Disappearance or Death of Family Member

20

ALMA GARRET

Intake Information: Client is a 30 year old female seeking therapy for help processing the recent death of her husband in a mining accident. Client reports feeling numb and detached from reality as she deals with grief, along with the pressure of taking over husband's business affairs, which are pressing. Client describes having recently moved from her hometown on the East Coast to a small frontier town out West, where her living situation and social life are drastically different than what she is accustomed to. Client is recently widowed, has no children, and indicates no previous therapy experience.

Alma Garrett sits on the couch across from me, wearing a long dress with layers of ruffles. Her hair is intricately braided and piled high on her head, and she occasionally dabs at her eyes with a tissue.

"I'm sorry for all the crying, I don't mean to make you uncomfortable," Alma says. "It's just that, the events of the past month have been quite difficult."

"That makes sense," I say. "And please, feel free to cry. In fact, I encourage it. You're here to talk about your husband's death. If there's any place where it's okay to cry, it's here."

"Thank you. Shall I continue with my story?"

"Please do."

"Very well." Alma sighs with the burden of recent events,

then continues. “It was quite a shock, but at the same time, I felt like something bad was on the horizon. Brom was happy back East, and his family was doing quite well, but with the panic of ’73 and subsequent financial crash, our finances became questionable, so he articulated this plan to come out West and find his fortune as a miner of gold. And I came along for the ride. A ride I didn’t choose to take, but it was pitched to me as a great opportunity. Of course, it was also supposed to help with my hysteria.”

“Hysteria?”

“Many women of my age, women of status in society, suffer from what the doctors call hysteria. This refers to an experience that is unique to women, and I’m sure you won’t mind if I don’t go into detail about it. That would be unladylike. That’s why my doctor prescribed me the tincture. Which helps.”

“What’s this tincture?”

“Laudanum. It’s a bit of a cure-all, a solution taken orally by dropper that mutes the pain of a woman’s natural biological experiences, among other things.”

I jot this down in my notes. “Sorry for asking so many questions, but what exactly is in this tincture?“

Alma starts to speak, then thinks better of it. “Might we focus our conversation on the death of my husband and the ensuing complications?”

I make note of Alma’s resistance, but don’t press her on it. “Of course, please, go on.”

“The honest truth about Brom is that he had great expectations, but he overestimated his own abilities,” she continues. “Although it was his stated goal to acquire his own fortune, he didn’t have a clue as to how to actually do it. You see, he was born to privilege, and never had to develop the personal qualities that most driven men have that were made unnecessary by his family’s wealth. And unfortunately, I suspect his naiveté is what led to his demise.”

"Could you tell me about what happened to Brom?"

Alma looks as if she'd like to avoid this part of the conversation, but carries on. "Well, in simple terms, we arrived in Deadwood, where Brom staked his claim and bought a plot of land, and mere weeks later, in a dreadful mining accident, he fell to his death. And now I, having been dragged along on this journey, find myself stuck in a town of ill repute, owner of a worthless plot of land, untrusting of my surroundings and uncertain about the future."

Alma goes on to describe her daily life in Deadwood. The run-down hotel she lives in, the unsavory characters around her, and the few people who seem to be on her intellectual level. Every now and then she dabs at her eyes with a lace handkerchief. I listen to her description of her experience of grief, but I can't stop thinking about her mention of laudanum, and how the use of it must color her entire experience of the situation.

"It was a brief affair, understated and unceremonious," Alma says, describing her husband's funeral. "A message was sent to his family back East, but with no working telegraph in Deadwood that will take weeks to arrive, and additional weeks to respond."

"And how are you handling the grief of his passing? I see you're able to cry, to express your emotions that way."

Alma thinks about this for a moment. "I feel... numb. Sometimes I wake up in that dirty hotel room and wonder where I am. It's confusing for a moment, like I'm in a dream and I expect to wake up back in New York, like none of this ever happened."

"You mentioned feeling numb. Could this also be an effect of the laudanum?"

Alma's expression shifts as she addresses this topic. "Yes, I believe that's one of the effects. One might call it numbness, but in truth it's a welcome respite from the natural ill feelings a woman experiences."

"I would imagine it's a welcome respite from many feelings, including grief and anxiety."

"Yes, I suppose." Alma shifts in her seat uncomfortably.

I wait to see if she'll continue, but she doesn't. "I believe laudanum has opium in it, is that correct?" I ask.

"I believe you're right, but this tincture is nothing like the scourge of opium that those Orientals traffic in. That's a dirty business, and sad really, those wretched souls who languish in opium dens, smoking their lives away. No, this tincture is a respectable medical treatment offered by university-trained doctors to patients of the upper class."

"And yet, the experience of having one's difficult experiences and feelings about them numbed seems to be a similarity in both experiences of the drug."

Alma reacts with defensiveness. "It's not a drug, it's medicine. And I'm not here to discuss my medical experiences. I'm here to discuss the death of my husband, and the resulting questions that event has raised."

Alma begins to share her plans for her future in Deadwood. She is considering selling her husband's land claim to a local bar owner, but something about the process makes her suspect it might not be worthless after all. She intends to reach out to an honorable man she met, a nearby hardware store owner, who she hopes will provide her with guidance about how to proceed with a business she is unfamiliar with.

I notice Alma begin to shiver as she speaks, crossing her arms around her.

"You look cold, Alma. Here, take this."

I offer her a blanket from a nearby chair.

"Thank you. Yes, I fear I do have the chills," she says as she arranges the blanket over her shoulders. Alma then begins to look through her purse, distracted. I sit and watch as she rifles through it, becoming agitated.

"I wonder if it's in my carriage..." she says out loud to herself.

"What is?"

"My tincture. It's a long, bumpy carriage ride back to Deadwood, and I intend to meet with interested parties tomorrow about the land claim."

I nod, take a breath, and then try to reintroduce the topic of her dependency on the tincture. "Alma, I want to share my observation that while you are here to discuss your husband's death and the aftermath, both emotionally and business-wise, I think your use of laudanum is also worth discussing."

Alma seems to feign ignorance. "What matter is that? It's completely normal. Many of my friends back East have the same experience."

"Would you say you've become dependent on this tincture?"

Alma sits up straight, her affect changing.

"I am offended by your line of questions, sir, and the implication that this medicine I use under the supervision of a doctor might be some kind of drug, the likes of which are used by the poor and indigent."

"Well, I'm sorry to offend you, but you see, clients come to see me for a variety of reasons, and the reasons they come for aren't the only ones worth discussing. There are also issues that we might not want to talk about, that we might avoid bringing up. In fact, the resistance we experience when broaching these subjects is often an indicator of their importance."

Alma looks at me with suspicion, and I try to project a friendly affect as I continue. "It's like when you have a massage. The masseuse might be working on your back and touch a sore spot that causes you to squirm and avoid because it's painful to touch. You might even tell the masseuse to avoid that area. And the masseuse would probably do that, and the massage would continue, but the masseuse would know that the sore spot, the most painful area to touch that you want to avoid the most, is actually the source of the pain that led you to get a massage in the first place, and it's only by working through the pain of that spot that real improvement can happen."

As I speak Alma seems to go through a range of emotions, from anger to acceptance to sadness.

"Does that make sense?" I ask.

Alma nods, resigned. "It does. And perhaps you're right. If I were to be truly honest with myself I might suspect that the use of the tincture is but a barrier to the engagement with matters far more important that I prefer to avoid. And this is something I agree might be worth discussing in future sessions. But I'm afraid we can't get into it now, I must go."

I join her as she stands, gathering her belongings, then turns to me.

"I can appreciate my reliance on the tincture might be both a salve to my current situation as well as a contributing factor," Alma says. "I can't say I look forward to discussing this in future sessions, but I recognize the fact that I must."

"I'm glad to hear that," I say. "I'll see you next week."

She exits, and I close the door behind her, then sit down to write up my notes.

Clinical Notes: Client presented with a muted affect, relating her experience of the death of her husband and the feelings of grief this has caused. Client described the circumstances that led her and husband to make the move from the East Coast to the small town of Deadwood, as well as the confusion she now finds herself in after his death as she struggles to resolve their financial arrangements. Client discussed her use of laudanum, leading Therapist to assess her dependence on it, something Client was resistant to. Therapist explained to Client the idea that this reliance on laudanum was something important to explore. Client was resistant at first, but eventually stated she would be willing to discuss topic further in future sessions.

Diagnosis:

F11.20: Opioid Dependence, Uncomplicated

Z63.4: Disappearance or Death of Family Member

21

TRAVIS BICKLE

Intake Information: Client is a 26 year old male seeking therapy for help with insomnia and depression. Client describes feelings of alienation and loneliness, and reports living a life isolated from social interaction and close relationships. Client's history includes serving in the military in Vietnam, and he currently lives in New York City, where he works as a taxi driver. Client is single, and reports no previous therapy experience.

Travis Bickle sits on the couch across from me with a stiff posture, hands on his thighs, his face emotionless, speaking in monotone.

"I work long hours. Six in the afternoon till six in the morning. Sometimes longer than that. I'll work fifteen, eighteen hour days. Seven days a week, most of the time. I don't mind, though. It keeps me busy."

"That is a pretty busy schedule. When do you sleep?" I ask.

"I don't sleep much. But it don't bug me. I just work more. It's better that way. I don't know what I'd do with idle time."

"How long have you been doing this?"

Travis thinks for a moment. "About a year. I sorta drifted around after I got back from Nam. Took a while for me to land in the city, and not long after that I got this job. I was struggling to find a place, you know? To fit in somewhere. I guess I found it."

"Tell me about your time in Vietnam."

Travis winces, and doesn't respond right away. He thinks about this before saying, "I don't want to talk about that."

I sense his defensiveness, and pause before replying.

"Okay, that's cool. I won't push you to talk about anything you don't want to talk about. I do have to say, though, that therapy is a place where people often end up talking about the things they would most like to avoid talking about."

Travis sits for a moment, processing this. We sit in silence for another moment as I wait to see if he'll open up. Then he does.

"Vietnam was hell. People dying left and right. Buddies of mine. Guys you were playing cards with the night before getting their heads blown off the next day. And then you'd go out and shoot up a village, kill everything that moves, thinking it'd make you feel better, but it didn't. It never did. The anger, man. There was so much of it. And it never went away."

"So, you still feel that anger?"

He laughs bitterly "Every day. Only instead of Viet Cong it's anger at the filth in this city. The whores, the beggars, the queens, fairies, dopers, junkies... Someday a real rain will come and wash all this scum off the streets."

This is a little concerning to me, so I don't respond right away, thinking of what to say. I decide to move the conversation in a new direction.

"Tell me about your social life," I say.

"My social life?" Travis seems surprised.

"Yeah. Any close friendships or romantic relationships?"

"No, I don't really have any relationships. I mean, I live in the city, I drive a cab, I talk to people all the time. But nothing more than where you headed, this is the fare, that kinda thing. I'm pretty much a loner."

"What do you like to do with the little free time you have? Any hobbies?"

"No. I just work. I wish I had something I liked to do. It

might give me a sense of purpose. As it is, I'm just wandering around the city, thinking about things."

"And what's your relationship like with drugs and alcohol?"

"Eh, I drink a little. Been taking some pills to help me stay awake. Those really work, let me tell you. It's so nice to just take a pill and feel better."

"Well Travis, I was actually going to suggest referring you to a psychiatrist to discuss the possibility of medication. It sounds like you're suffering from clinical depression. Your insomnia, social isolation, anger, these are all classic symptoms. And while a pill isn't going to be a cure-all that just makes all the bad feelings go away, for many clients antidepressants can help lift the burden of serious depression off their shoulders in a way that allows them to live their lives without this dark cloud following them around."

Travis seems intrigued. "So, it's pills?"

"Yes."

"And they'll make me feel better?"

"They might."

"They won't mess with my head, will they?"

"Well, there could be side effects, but that's something you would discuss with the psychiatrist."

"What do I tell them?"

"You just tell them what we talked about here, and they'll take it from there."

Travis thinks for a moment, then nods. "Okay, let's do it."

CUT TO:

Six weeks later. I haven't seen Travis since our last session. He's sitting on the couch across from me, dressed in the same clothes as last time, but now he has a much different affect. He's upbeat, with a newfound warmth. And he has a new haircut: a mohawk.

"Dr. Velez was really great, thanks for referring me to her," Travis says with a friendly tone. "We talked about my depression, and she recommended an anti-depressant, which I started taking, but nothing happened, so she put me on another one, and at first it was the same thing, no difference. But then it got worse. Like, things got really dark. I started thinking some pretty scary thoughts. I even gave myself this crazy haircut. It made sense at the time. So I called Dr. Velez with these concerns, and she adjusted my dosage. Then things get a little better, not so dark, but then one day, about a week later, I woke up and things were just... different. It felt like a heavy blanket had been lifted off my shoulders. I was happy. Which was a weird feeling, you know? So unfamiliar. I could't remember the last time I felt happy. So, I wouldn't say the pill just made all my problems go away, but it definitely made me feel less depressed."

Travis sits back, smiling now, marveling at his journey.

"I'm so glad you had a positive experience," I say. "Those kind of medications work differently for different people, so I'm not surprised to hear that it took a couple of attempts until you noticed a difference. And Dr. Velez explained all this to you?"

"Oh yeah, she was a saint putting up with me. I wasn't exactly easy to deal with at first. I have to admit, I was sort of a basket case."

I jot this down in my notes. "And how else have things changed for you?"

"Well, I'm actually sleeping now. In fact, I had to cut back on work because I can't stay up for twenty-four hours at a time anymore. And I feel less angry now. I find myself being nicer to people. Like, I'll look in the rearview mirror and notice I'm smiling. I'm smiling! And I don't even know why." He shakes his head in pleasant disbelief.

"It sounds like the medication has helped mitigate some of the depression you were carrying around. And by the way, that's a subject that I think we should continue to explore here. Because while the pill might have helped you right off the bat, it's the underlying issues, the anger, your experiences in the war and how they stay with you today, that we need to process in order to get you to a place where you don't need the pills to live a happy life."

"Yeah, I get that. And I'm okay with it."

"Great. Well, we're just about out of time for today, but we can pick back up with this topic next week."

"Sounds good," says Travis cheerfully. "Thanks!"

I rise to open the office door for Travis to exit, and as he crosses out I feel my phone vibrate in my pocket. "Oops, forgot to put you on Do Not Disturb" I mutter as I decline the call.

Travis stops and turns around.

"You talking to me?"

"No, just my phone."

"Oh, okay. See you next week!"

Travis smiles warmly and exits. I close the door behind him, then sit down to write up my notes.

Clinical Notes: Client presented with a flat affect, describing symptoms of what Therapist suspected might be clinical depression. Client related his experience serving in Vietnam, detailing the trauma of seeing his friends killed, and himself killing enemy soldiers in return, and describing symptoms of PTSD. Client expressed interest in medication, so Therapist referred Client to psychiatrist, and Client was prescribed medication that helped with his depression. After this, Client displayed a friendly affect, describing a new state of happiness, and was able to discuss his depression in the past tense. Client expressed his appreciation for the value of seeing a psychiatrist, and indicated his openness to continuing in talk therapy treatment.

Diagnosis:

F32.3: Major Depressive Disorder, Recurrent, Severe with Psychotic Features

F43.10: Post-Traumatic Stress Disorder, Unspecified

22

MIKE AND CAROL BRADY

Intake Information: Clients are a 36 year old male and a 35 year old female who are recently married. They each have three children from previous marriages, making this a large blended family, and are in the process of adjusting to this new arrangement. Clients seek couples therapy to help with conflict around their different parenting styles, especially in terms of gender roles and expectations. Clients have no previous therapy experience.

Mike and Carol Brady sit on the couch across from me, looking very much like a happily married couple. They compliment each other well, and are just plain cheerful.

"We met through mutual friends," recounts Carol. "I had just gotten divorced, and Mike's wife had recently passed."

"We hit it off right away," continues Mike. "Here was this lovely lady, raising three very lovely girls, who all had beautiful golden blonde hair, just like their mother."

"And Cindy with her curls," reminisces Carol, who smiles back at him. "And Mike was busy with three boys of his own. They were four men living all together."

"But in a way, we were all alone," observes Mike.

"And the moment we met, I just had this hunch. I knew this group would somehow form a family." Carol takes Mike's hand, and they share a smile.

"Sounds like a big bunch," I observe. "How has it been, this experience of adjusting to living together under one roof? I would imagine there have been some growing pains."

"Oh, every week it's another zany situation," says Mike. "But one thing that has been a constant during our first year together is, we're realizing we have very different parenting styles."

I nod and jot this down in my notes. "That makes sense. When you're a single parent, you have 100% of the parenting responsibility. You get to make all the decisions. But now that you've combined your families, and you each have a partner again, you have to learn how to share those duties again."

"That's absolutely right," says Carol. "But we find ourselves butting heads over this. For instance, I think Mike is too hard on the boys. He's coaching them in baseball, and I think he's too much of a drill sergeant with them."

"And I think Carol is too permissive with the girls," replies Mike. "She coddles them, and lets them get away with everything."

"I see. And how has this frustration shown up in your relationship?"

Mike and Carol look to each other, considering this.

"How has this shown up in our relationship?" repeats Carol, thinking. "Well, I'm less likely to be nice to him when he comes home from work. I have to admit, I can get a little snappy."

"And I'm less likely to ask her about her day after I come home from work," admits Mike. "I guess I can be a little less warm, you know?"

"And what about the kids? I'm wondering what their experience has been like. Have they verbalized any complaints about your respective parenting styles?"

"No, I don't know if they've even noticed," observes Carol.

"But we certainly have," says Mike. "I just can't help but think the girls would be better served with some firmer parenting. Higher expectations, stronger rules."

"And I wonder if the boys would appreciate some gentler parenting. More flexibility, more discussion."

"This is interesting. And I just had a zany idea." I lean forward to make my pitch. "What if you two swapped places? Meaning Carol, you took the boys to practice one week, and Mike you stayed home with the girls."

They look to each other, intrigued.

"Now don't feel like this is something you have to do," I say. "I understand if it sounds too sitcom-y."

"No, I like that idea," says Mike. "What do you think, Carol?"

"I think it's a great idea. I'd like to try being a baseball coach. Touchdown!"

As Mike shakes his head, I hear the sound of an audience laughing from out of nowhere. Before I can ask them about it, my vision becomes blurry.

DISSOLVE TO:

I find myself sitting in my office chair again, with Mike and Carol sitting on the couch across from me again.

"That was a great suggestion you made, Phil, for us to swap parenting roles for the week," says Mike.

"Yes," agrees Carol. "It was awkward at first, but there were some laughs and funny moments, and a little bit of drama, and in the end we all learned a valuable lesson."

"That's great to hear," I say. "So, tell me about the experience. How was it for you, Carol?"

"I'll just say this: Mike can keep his job as baseball coach. I didn't realize how important it is in sports to have the kind of drill sergeant attitude he has. I tried to approach the boys with gentle support and positivity, and they didn't really respond to that at first. But I got the sense they appreciated that I had actually done the research and was able to help them with some of the technical aspects of baseball. I showed them that I wasn't the typical girl they're used to who's afraid to get her hands dirty. By the end they were actually calling me coach!"

"So it sounds like it was a positive experience?" I ask.

"Oh definitely. Although one thing I definitely learned from all this is that I can't hit a curveball."

"Or any ball," adds Mike.

Again I hear the disembodied audience laugh, but before I can mention it, Mike continues.

"Well, my experience started out as a disaster. When I tried to talk to the girls with the same direct, honest approach I use with the boys, it didn't help them at all. Turns out women appreciate emotional empathy more than cold hard facts. And then we tried baking a pie, where I naturally applied the rigor and logic I use in my job as an architect, but it failed miserably, creating a complete mess in the kitchen. Which I cleaned up."

"And then later I cleaned up the clean-up," chimes in Carol.

"But the funny thing is, even though things didn't turn out the way I'd planned, I think the girls appreciated my effort," Mike continue. "Seeing me struggle with what I had thought were simple issues seemed to humanize me in their eyes, and it ended up being a memorable bonding experience."

"Last night before bed Cindy actually told me she enjoyed her time with you," shares Carol. "Her exact quote was 'Daddy's funny.'"

"I'm so glad to hear it turned out well," I say. "So, after this experience, how do you feel about each other's parenting styles?"

"I have to admit, I appreciate Carol's more gentle approach with the girls now. I can see how it might be exactly what they need."

"And I can see why Mike's drill sergeant approach is something the boys respond to, even if I think they did appreciate my different perspective."

"So, no desire to get each other to change their ways?"

Mike and Carol look to each other, considering this.

"It's funny. That's what I wanted at first, to see Carol change her parenting style. But now I see that it was really me who needed to change."

"And I thought if Mike parented the boys like I parent the girls we'd all be happier, but now I see that it's actually the opposite."

"What wonderful symmetry!" I observe. "It's so nice when a couple comes in with an issue, we explore it, consider how it might change, make some effort to create that change, and then arrive in a place where the issues are resolved."

"Yeah, that seems to happen to us a lot," admits Carol.

"Excellent, and I think that's a good place to end our session for today," I say, closing my notebook and rising to open the office door for them.

"Perfect timing, we need to get home early. Alice wants the night off," says Carol to Mike. "She and Sam are going to the movies."

"Do think they're, you know, an 'item'?" asks Mike.

Mike and Carol consider this for a moment, then say, at the same time: "Nah."

I hear the disembodied audience laugh again. "Do you guys hear that laughing sound?" I ask.

"Yeah, sorry about that," says Mike. "It follows us wherever we go."

"You get used to it," says Carol. "See you next week!"

As they exit the laugh track hits again, this time along with some hooting and applause.

I close the door behind them, then sit down to write up my notes.

. . .

Clinical Notes: Clients presented with engaged affects, sitting close to each other and displaying affection during session. Clients are a married couple with a large blended family, and struggle to support each other's parenting style. At Therapist's suggestion, Clients spent a week swapping parenting responsibilities. After this experience Clients indicated a new appreciation for each other's parenting styles, and reassessed their desires to see each other change their ways.

Diagnosis:

Z63.0: Relationship Distress with Spouse or Partner

Z63.5: Disruption of Family by Separation or Divorce

23

MICHAEL ROBINAVITCH

Intake Information: Client is a 54 year old male seeking therapy for help processing the death of a colleague. Client is also experiencing significant stress related to his job as an emergency room doctor. Client describes working long hours, having to make "difficult life and death decisions," and struggling with symptoms of PTSD on an everyday basis. Client is single, has no children, and indicates no previous therapy experience.

Michael Robinavitch sits on the couch across from me, wearing a leather motorcycle jacket with blue medical scrubs visible beneath it. A backpack and a motorcycle helmet sit on the couch next to him.

"I appreciate you seeing me this early in the morning, Phil," he says.

"It's no problem, Robert," I reply. "The older I get, the earlier I wake up."

"Please, call me Robby And I'm right there with you. Although the job is starting to take its toll on me. Emergency room work really is a young man's game."

"Yes, I saw in your paperwork that you're an emergency room doctor. Am I correct in assuming that's a pretty stressful job?"

He lets out a sharp laugh. "You assume correctly. It is

extremely stressful. A constant state of red alert. I experience daily the kind of stress most people are lucky to only experience a few times in their lives, and I do it fifteen hours a day, four days a week."

"That sounds like a lot. How do you handle that stress?"

"I compartmentalize. I also detach. Sometimes it's like I'm outside myself, watching me do my job. I also constantly joke about the most serious things a human being could possibly experience. Gallows humor, to use a clinical term. I'm sure you see this type of thing all the time with people who work in stressful environments, right?"

I nod. "Compartmentalizing, detachment, humor, they're all defense mechanisms, strategies people rely on to deal with stressful work environments, but also with any kind of repetitive stress, really. So that's normal."

"That's reassuring. But let me get to the reason I'm here."

He takes a deep breath and leans in, rubbing his hands together.

"Today isn't a regular today. Today is the four year anniversary of the death of a dear friend, co-worker, and mentor. A guy who was like a father to me. Which is why I've taken this day off from work every year since it happened. Until today. Today, I'm going in."

I sit quietly but attentively, waiting to see if Robby will continue. Eventually, he does.

"As a doctor, I have to make difficult decisions. Life or death, it's as simple as that. And there are an infinite number of decisions that build up to the big decisions. Over the many years I've been doing this, the thing I've come to appreciate the most, more than all the medical knowledge and experience I've accumulated, is the struggle to make those difficult choices based on facts rather than emotions. And four years ago on this day, I had to make that kind of choice."

Robby starts to tear up a bit. I have to remind myself not to jump in and say anything, but rather to let him tell his story at his own pace. After a quiet moment, he continues.

"Monty was my mentor. He taught me how to be a doctor. He also taught me how to be a human being. He led by example. So of course, when COVID hit, he was in the hospital every minute he was awake, and most of the minutes he was asleep. He caught it pretty early on. We did everything we could for him, just like we did for everybody. He ended up on an ECMO unit."

Robby notices my lack of recognition.

"Extracorporeal Membrane Oxygenation," he continues. "It's a device that basically pumps your blood for you, keeps you alive. It was a common intervention at that time for COVID patients with acute respiratory distress syndrome. But it wasn't going to help. He wasn't going to get any better. But at least he was alive."

Robby shakes his head and rubs his scalp. I can feel his stress. "That was such a crazy time. We were running at two hundred percent capacity, and even though Monty was alive, keeping him there was preventing another patient who needed that bed more from getting it. So I had to make one of those difficult life and death choices. I chose to take him off the machine. And that's what I did. And then, he died."

Robby chokes up as he says this, and the tears start to flow.

I push the box of Kleenex on the coffee table towards him, and he takes one, wipes his eyes, blows his nose.

"So yeah, it's going to be a hard day. And I figured this would be the perfect thing to talk to a therapist about."

"I have to agree. How do you feel after telling me all this?"

Robby thinks, making an assessment. "Slightly better. As a medical professional, I know that crying is an effective intervention. 'It's all right to cry' and all that."

"Rosey Grier, classic," I reply.

"Spot on, Phil. So there's that. I'm just concerned with how I'm going to feel walking into work today. How I'm going to react. If I'm going to be able to do my job." Now Robby looks to me, wanting my input.

"I suspect it might be hard," I say. "You're probably going to feel some pretty strong emotions."

"Right. I guess what I'm really worried about is... What if I freeze up? What if I have a panic attack? What if I can't function?"

I nod in understanding as I consider this. "I think it's natural to have that concern. And if it happens, there are things you can do to help. I can share some breathing exercises with you, but I wonder if, because of your profession, you're already familiar with some?"

"Sure, box breathing, sensory grounding, I know the drill. And I'll keep that in mind. I guess, for me, it's less about what I do if it happens and more about the fear that it will happen." He leans back on the couch with a sigh. I take the opportunity to move the conversation in a different direction.

"What do you do when you're not working?"

"I work on my bike." He raps knuckles on the motorcycle helmet next to him. "Do you ride?"

"No, I've never been interested in motorcycles. I don't really do anything that requires a helmet."

"Smart policy. I don't know, there's something about a motorcycle that just calls to me. Both being on the bike, and working on it when I'm not. Rebuilding a carburetor is like surgery, only it's not life or death, there are no emotions involved. I can turn that part of my brain off. There are no moral consequences for the choices you make about a carburetor."

"And what does it feel like when you're out there riding?"

Robby's affect brightens now. "It's great. It's just me and the road. There's nobody else to account for, nobody else to consider, no patients, no nurses, no charts, no sirens. Well, hopefully no sirens."

I chuckle. "Right."

"And the sound of the engine, the wind whistling through the helmet, I find it peaceful. Meditative. I'd call it my happy place, but it's not really happiness I'm experiencing. It's... peacefulness."

I watch him experience these positive emotions for a moment, then continue. "You know, Robby, as you talk about what you love about riding your motorcycle, your mood seemed to lighten. You seem at peace."

Robby nods as he appreciates this. "Yeah, I feel better after talking about it."

"Have you ever thought about taking some time off from work to do some kind of motorcycle trip? I mean, is that even a thing?"

"Hell yeah, it's a thing. But I've never really considered it, I'm just happy to cruise the Red Belt late at night when there's no traffic."

Then Robby cocks his head as he entertains a new thought. "But now that we're talking about it, maybe I should take a biking trip. I've always wanted to ride through the Badlands, on one of those highways that seems to stretch on forever. Not talk to anyone for a whole day, just me and my thoughts. Man, that sounds great."

"Maybe you should consider planning a trip?"

"Oh I can't, with work the way it is. I can't commit to something like that right now."

"Okay, but you don't have to commit to anything. Don't let yourself skip to the end result and use that as an excuse not to get started. Just do a little research, see how it feels. No pressure."

Robby nods as he appreciates this. "Yeah, okay. I can do that."

"And in terms of going back to work, we can talk about breathing exercises to help center you and reduce tension, but it sounds like what really helps is thinking about being on your motorcycle, riding through the desert on that deserted highway."

"It really does help," Robby chuckles. "Okay, that'll be a good visualization exercise for me today. If things go south. Or rather, when things go south. Because if there's one thing I've learned working in the ER, it's that things go south."

Just then the sound of sirens appears in the distance, growing louder as they approach.

Robby tenses up, looking out my office window.

Then his phone pings. He grabs it and reads a message. "Multi-car pile up on 376. Looks like we're going to have to cut this short."

"No problem, I understand," I say, as I rise to open the office door for him.

Robby grabs his stuff. "But thanks a lot, this has really helped."

"Glad to hear it. I'm here if you want to continue. And good luck today!"

But Robby is already gone.

I close the door behind him, then sit down to write up my notes.

Clinical Notes: Client presented with a friendly but serious affect, describing his work experience as an emergency room doctor, and sharing that reason for seeking therapy is to process grief related to the death of a mentor and work colleague. Client revealed that today is the four year anniversary of mentor's death, and he had always taken that day off until now, and is concerned about how he will react at work. Therapist and Client discussed interventions to help mitigate his anticipated stress and anxiety, and also explored Client's hobby of riding his motorcycle. This is a source of pleasure and peace for Client, and he intends to draw from these feelings to help mitigate his work stress.

Diagnosis:

F43.10: Post-Traumatic Stress Disorder, Unspecified
Z63.4: Disappearance or Death of Family Member

24

ADAM FRANKENSTEIN

Intake Information: Client is a 40 year old male seeking therapy to address conflict with father. Client describes a turbulent relationship with father, and a vague personal history, including a timeline that seems to indicate Client was born within the last year, but refers to his age as 40. Client describes an intense antipathy for father, yet also a strong desire for validation and support from him, something he describes his father as being incapable of providing. Client is single, and indicates no previous therapy experience.

Adam Frankenstein sits on the couch across from me, a large man wearing a dirty cloak and muddy boots, with pale, greenish skin, and scars crisscrossing his misshapen face. He sits stiffly on the couch, looking uncomfortable.

"You may call me Adam," he says, with a melancholic tone. "I am the second first man, made in the image of my creator."

"I see," I say as I jot this down in my notes. "And when you say creator, are you referring to your father?"

"I am indeed. He is the man who is responsible for my existence, and who I blame for the misery I wallow in every day of my short but tortuous waking life."

I sit with Adam in his sadness, waiting to see if he'll continue. He doesn't, so I do.

"It's common for there to be conflict with our parents, and

more specifically, in your case, between fathers and sons," I say. "And that kind of conflict can certainly result in sadness and depression. You indicated in your intake paperwork that you're adopted?"

Adam sighs. "It's complicated. I said adopted because I wanted to make sure you knew that my father is not my birth father. Although I am created in his image. I don't know whether to call him my father or my creator, or simply by his name, Victor. Victor Frankenstein."

Suddenly thunder booms outside my office window, which is weird because the weather is calm and sunny.

I turn back to Adam. "Okay, we have several options for how to refer to him. In my line of work we sometimes refers to parents as caregivers, which takes the emphasis away from gender or genetic considerations, and focuses on the fact that these people, however we call them, are the ones who cared for us when we were young, and who modeled for us the behavior that is often the reason we seek therapy."

Adam nods in agreement. "Well said. Then yes, he is my caregiver. And even though I hate him with all my heart, I still consider him my father, biological or not."

"Then let's just call him father. So, Adam, tell me about your relationship with your father."

Adam chuckles slightly. "What about my father? Well, I blame him for my predicament. My lot in life. I did not ask to be born! Yet he created me, and then abandoned me."

"When you say abandoned, are we talking about emotional abandonment?" I ask. "Physical abandonment? What did this abandonment look like?"

"Twas both physical and emotional. And I know not which pains me the most. My father brought me into this world, a newborn, a defenseless creature with no idea how to walk, and after he saw how I was, how I looked, how I sounded, he gave up on me. It's like I was just one big failure in his eyes."

Adam starts to tear up. I push the box of Kleenex towards him.

"Thanks," says Adam, dabbing at his tears. "My father spent so many years of his life obsessively working towards my creation, so single minded and determined, and yet in the moment I drew my first breath he completely reversed course. He never supported me emotionally, and physically he preferred to hope I would simply disappear. So I left. Is it so wrong to seek love, Phil?"

"Not at all. Is that what you want from your father?"

"Yes! I want to be loved. And yet all I get is disgust. Repulsion. Hatred."

Adam sits with these feelings, sadness mixed with anger. I wait for a moment, then ask another question.

"What was your father's childhood like?"

Adam looks surprised. "What do you query me thus? Shouldn't we limit our talk to the topic at hand?"

"I know it seems off track, but I find that understanding what our parents' relationship was like with their parents, how they were programmed to act by them, can inform how we interact with our parents in our relationships," I say. "An exploration of their history can shed some light on the reasons and motivations behind their actions."

Adam looks doubtful but game. "Very well, then. What was my father's childhood like? I know his father was a cruel man who cared little for my father's feelings and emotions, and instead used his unreachable expectations as a shield against the love one might expect a father to feel for a son. My father was never able to live up to his father's expectations."

"And it sounds like your father has a similar approach to his relationship with you?"

"Indeed. I never met my father's father, but I can see his image in my father. Not the image of his face, but the image of his cowardice. His coldness. My father is just a child playing at being a god, because his own father never let him be a man."

"That's very insightful, Adam," I say, impressed.

"Thanks," he replies. "I've thought about this a lot."

"So now we can clearly see how your father's relationship with you was informed less by you and more by his own father. Tell me about his mother. Your grandmother."

Adam laughs bitterly. "My father's mother was the only one who protected him, who was an emotional buffer to his tyrant of a father. And she died a slow, painful death, from a protracted illness. She was his only advocate, and she was taken from him prematurely. And this is what led him to vow to take the act of the creation of life away from the realm of our creator and conquer it himself. To defeat death."

I write this down as I reply. "Defeat death. An interesting metaphor, even if it's impossible."

"Oh, you'd be surprised. My father is a brilliant man. Even if I have come to consider that this brilliance has made him even more of a monster than me."

"Well, now we can see how your father acted towards you in exactly the way he was programmed to act by his own parents. If his father never showed him how to be a loving, supportive parent, we can understand that he's not equipped to be that way with you. Even though it's something you seem to want very badly, something we all might need and crave."

"I can appreciate that. Oh, how his love could have made me a gentle giant, but alas, his rejection hath made me a mean monster."

"And have you had a conversation with your father where you were able to say all this to him?" I ask. "Where you expressed all these feelings you're sharing with me?"

"Not in so many words. We have yet to have a final show-down. But the chase is on. He's a hard guy to pin down. And I'm afraid that even if I were able to corner him he would simply refuse to have this discussion. To acknowledge these feelings that I so clearly express to you."

"You know, there's an approach to this that I find sometimes helps clients dealing with issues related to their relationship with their parents. It's called the Unsent Letter. Basically, this entails the client writing a letter to their parent, sharing in clear, unambiguous detail their feelings about them, about their childhood, their frustration with their relationship, their anger, their pain, almost like a diary entry, but organized and thought out. It's a way to get all these feelings we're feeling inside out of us and into the world in a way that sometimes helps us process these feelings, and maybe even move on from them."

Adam seems intrigued. "So, similar to what we are discussing here in terms of content?"

"Yes, but written in your own hand. Or typed."

"And yet you describe this letter as unsent?"

"Right, because after doing this, after getting all these feelings out onto paper, we can look at it and realize that the letter isn't really for our parent. It's for us. Because it's not like our parent will read this letter and say 'Oh, I get it now, I understand what you're going through, and I'm here to tell you I'm going to change and become a better parent, the kind of parent you wanted and deserved.' That's a fairy tale response that we'll never get."

"Yes, 'tis a fairy tale, indeed."

"What we would most likely get in response instead is more anger, more conflict, more resentment, more of what we're already experiencing," I continue. "So yes, the letter ends up being unsent, but the act of writing it is where the real healing begins."

"I see. It seems this act might suffice to empower myself to be responsible for my own happiness. To quell my desire for revenge. By sharing my pain I might lessen the desire to see that pain shared by others."

"Exactly."

Adam thinks for a moment, then asks: "How shall I begin?"

"Begin at the beginning. Don't worry about editing yourself. Just let yourself write. Whatever you come up with, we can review next week, and edit until you have something you feel truly describes how you feel."

Adam nods, determined now. "I shall endeavor to write this letter. Although I know not how to wield a quill. But I do know of voice dictation. I shall ask Siri."

Adam pulls an iPhone out of his pocket.

"Siri, create a Notes document called 'Letter to Father.'"

Siri replies: "Calling Father."

"No! Dang it." Adam panics, fumbling with his phone, cancelling the call.

I cross over to open the office door for Adam. "See you next week?"

"Yes, you shall," says Adam as he exits.

I close the door behind him, then sit down to write up my notes.

Clinical Notes: Client presented with a melancholic affect, as he described frustration with relationship with father, expressing feelings of being unwanted and unloved. Therapist and Client examined this relationship, as well as father's relationship with his parents, in an effort to learn more about why Client's father acts as he does in their relationship. Therapist described the Unsent Letter intervention as a way to externalize Client's feelings about father, and to develop a greater understanding of the folly of expecting father to change. Client responded positively to this intervention, and intends to complete it in order to review letter in session next week.

. . .

Diagnosis:

F43.21: Adjustment Disorder with Depressed Mood

Z62.821: Parent-Adopted Child Conflict

25

JESSE MONTGOMERY III AND CHESTER GREENBERG

Intake Information: Clients are 22 year old males who seek therapy to address concerns about cannabis use. Clients describe near constant use of cannabis, including a recent bender that was so intense that there were unable to find their car afterwards, and which provided motivation for them to reach out for therapy. Clients are both single, and report no previous therapy experience.

Jesse and Chester sit on the couch across from me, turned to face each other, in the middle of an argument.

"Sweet! What did mine say?" asks Jesse.

"Dude! What about mine?" replies Chester.

"Sweet! What did mine say?" asks Jesse.

"Dude! What about mine?" replies Chester.

"Sweet! What did mine say?" asks Jesse.

"Dude! What about mine?" replies Chester.

"Sweet! What did mine say?" asks Jesse.

"Dude! What about mine?" replies Chester.

"Sweet! What did mine say?" asks Jesse.

"Dude! What about mine?" replies Chester.

I finally have to break up the conversation. "Guys, listen." I point to Jesse. "Your tattoo said 'dude.'" Then I point to Chester. "Your tattoo said 'sweet.' Got it?"

Jesse and Chester look confused, then turn back to each other, and finally nod as they get it.

"Dude!" says Jesse.

"Sweet!" says Chester.

They share a childish giggle.

I attempt to get the session back on track. "Let's get back to the topic at hand. The reason for you dudes coming here. This concern about your use of cannabis."

"Canna-who?" Chester looks confused.

"He means shibby, dude," says Jesse.

"How'd you come up with that word, shibby?" I ask.

"Oh, it was just a silly word we made up in high school to refer to marijuana so nobody would know what we were talking about," says Jesse.

"But it turns out everyone knew what we were talking about anyways," says Chester. "I don't know how they cracked the code. But we liked the word, and it stuck."

"I can see that," I say. "It does sound friendlier than cannabis. And you should feel free to continue to use that word, but I will probably still refer to it as cannabis."

"Canna-who?" Chester looks confused.

"He means shibby, dude," says Jesse.

"Tell me about your relationship with cannabis. Or, shibby."

"Our relationship?" Jesse asks, then considers this. "Well, I'd say we're very close. Like, we're married."

"We met in middle school, and we instantly fell in love," Chester continues. "It became our thing. Like, we always wanted to be shibbied. All day, all night, all the time."

"And it was pretty sweet back then, in high school," says Jesse. "We got okay grades, we made it through and graduated, but the whole time we were using shibby more and more."

"And after graduation, we started using it a lot more and more," admits Chester. "Like, from the moment we woke up to the moment we fell asleep. We had some jobs on and off, and thought about going to college, but we were too busy having fun. Shibby, right?"

"But then recently things came to a head with this crazy night we had, where we got so shibbied the night before that the next morning we couldn't remember where we parked our car. And that was scary," says Jesse.

"Yeah. Along with the aliens and the continuum transfunctioner and the whole saving the universe thing," says Chester. "But not being able to remember where we parked the car, that's what really motivated us to reach out to you."

"Even though we ended up finding the car. Sorry, spoiler alert."

"It's okay, I wrote the movie," I say. "Okay, let's do this. I'll ask you some questions intended to measure the intensity of your cannabis use, so we can get a better idea about your usage. Sound good?"

The dudes nod in agreement.

"Okay," I continue. "First question: Have you ever found yourself using more cannabis during a session than intended?"

The dudes answer at the same time: "Yes."

"Have you ever tried to cut back on your cannabis use but not been able to?"

"Yes."

"Has your use of cannabis ever created conflict in your relationships?"

"Yes."

"Have there been times when you skipped social or work engagements because—"

Yes."

"Have you ever found yourself in a situation where—"

"Yes."

"Have you ever—"

"Yes."

I stop writing their answers down. "Okay, I think that's—"

"Yes."

"Actually, the assessment is over—"

"Yes."

"No, that's it—"

"Yes."

"We're done!" I say a bit too loudly, trying not to get frustrated with the dudes.

"How'd we do?" asks Chester.

"Let's just say you tested positive for shibby."

"Sweet! Wait, is that good?" asks Jesse.

"Not exactly," I say. "It seems to me that you guys use cannabis to the point of abuse, where it's affecting your lives in a negative way. And it's taken awhile, but you've finally gotten to the point where you'd like to see that change. Is that accurate?"

"Absolutely. But, we don't want to just quit," says Jesse. "Shibby is a part of our lives. It's a part of us."

"Yeah, we are one with the shibby, and the shibby is one with us," says Chester. "We couldn't imagine never using shibby again."

"But the idea of quitting is just as scary as the idea of continuing with how things are now," says Jesse, as if realizing this for the first time. "It's like, a conundrum."

"I don't know," counters Chester. "To me, it's more like a confusing and difficult problem or question."

I sit with the dudes as they consider this, then continue. "Why don't you tell me what you would imagine the perfect outcome to be. Like, if you could choose exactly how you'd like your relationship with cannabis to be in the future, what would that look like?"

The dudes sit back and think for a moment, then Jesse shares his thoughts.

"I think about us going to college. Getting degrees. Becoming professionals. Businessmen. Getting jobs, investing in the stock market, opening retirement accounts, becoming reliable partners for our girlfriends, maybe even starting families."

Chester chimes in. "And being able to find our car."

"Yeah, that would be sweet."

"And where does cannabis fit in your lives in this scenario?"

"It's still there," says Chester. "But it's not a problem. Like, we might use it on the weekends. Or at a concert. Or if we're hanging out with large breasted aliens who want to give us oral pleasure. But definitely not before work. And definitely not before our weddings."

"Yeah. Dude, where's my wedding ring? Hey, that could be the sequel!" says Jesse, then turns to me. "Why wasn't there ever a sequel?"

"It's a long story. Right now, let's concentrate on what we're doing here," I say. "Tell me more about how your cannabis use affects your relationship with your girlfriends."

The dudes both shake their heads unhappily. "It's not good dude," says Jesse. "It seems like we're always trying to prove that we're good boyfriends, but it's hard because we're always shibbied, and it's the way we act and the things we do when we're shibbied that are the things that our girlfriend don't like about us."

"Yeah. We forget things. We're inconsiderate. And we forget things. And we're inconsiderate," says Chester.

"We're also forgetful and inconsistent," adds Jesse. "Clearly we would be better boyfriends if it wasn't for all the shibby."

"That makes sense," I say. "The abuse of any substance or activity can create a barrier to intimacy that, no matter how hard you work to break down, will always be there as long as the abuse is there."

"So that's another reason to quit," says Jesse.

"Quit? Like, forever? I don't know, dude. That's scary!" says Chester, who then turns to me. "Do we have to quit?"

"I don't know, but I do know that you don't have to decide

now. The important thing now, right here, is that you can acknowledge that your use of cannabis is affecting your lives in a negative way, and you want to change that. It doesn't have to be all or nothing, at least right now. You can take it one day at a time. Try not use cannabis for a day. See how it feels. It'll probably be a struggle, and you'll probably end up using cannabis again. And then you'll try stopping again. It will be a cycle, a process, and it will probably last a long time."

"That sounds like a cycle that's probably going to last for a long time," says Jesse mournfully.

"I agree, but starting that cycle will lead to progress along the path from where you are now to where you want to be," I say. "I mean, this ideal life you just described for yourself sounds pretty sweet. Where your use of cannabis is not abuse, where it has less power over you. Where it takes up less of your mental energy, to the point where you don't even think about it. And you're able to dedicate yourselves to your relationships and your careers in a way that's positive and productive, and not in conflict with your relationship with cannabis."

"Canna-who?" asks Chester.

"Shibby," I say, as I sneak a look at the clock. "Now, we're just about out of time for today. I'll see you guys next week, same time?"

"Yes, for sure. Should we try not to partake of any shibby until then?"

"That's up to you. If it feels good, try not to. And if you can't, track how you feel when you do use shibby, and we can talk about that."

I cross over and open the door for the guys as they exit my office. "Do you remember where you parked?" I ask them.

"Oh, we took a Waymo," says Jesse. "It drives itself, dude!"

"Shotgun!" yells Chester, as the dudes rush out.

I close the door behind them, then sit down to write up my notes.

. . .

Clinical Notes: Clients presented with engaged affects, eager to discuss their relationship with cannabis and goals for changing it. Clients described a long-time relationship with cannabis, and how its use is ingrained in their everyday lives and personalities. However, Clients seem motivated to change that, and describe a future where their career goals and relationships become their focus without the distraction of cannabis use. Clients are resistant to completely eliminating cannabis from their lives, and Therapist supported them in the knowledge that it will not happen all at once, but with effort and intention they will be able to live the lives and have the relationships with their partners and with cannabis that they want.

Diagnosis:

F12.20: Cannabis Dependence, Uncomplicated

F44.0: Dissociative Amnesia

RESOURCES

There are various online databases you can use to find a therapist. They're similar to online dating apps. They present profiles that can help you narrow the field and choose people you'd like to learn more about.

Psychology Today - www.psychologytoday.com/us

Psychology Today is the largest, most comprehensive online database of mental health professionals, with filters to help you refine your search by location, area of expertise, price, and insurance. Make sure to check out my profile!

www.psychologytoday.com/us/therapists/phil-stark-los-angeles-ca/879165

TherapyDen - www.therapyden.com

TherapyDen has a smaller database than Psychology Today, but has an emphasis on helping you find therapists who share your values and worldview (I'm on there too).

www.therapyden.com/therapist/phil-stark-los-angeles-ca

There are also platforms that will help you find a therapist who specifically takes your insurance, and make it easier to deal with the billing and verification process.

headway.co

helloalma.com

growtherapy.com

Perhaps the best way to find the right therapist, however, is through a personal recommendation. The kind you might get from a friend or family member. Of course, this would entail you actually saying to a friend or family member that you are looking for a therapist, which can be scary and perhaps embarrassing as you admit that your life is not picture-prefect. This approach requires courage and an embrace of vulnerability.

I encourage you to try this! You might get a great referral to a therapist you hit it off with, and by introducing this topic to friends or family members, you might end up having a meaningful discussion about the personal experience of issues and events that might lead one to seek therapy for support. You might learn things about your friends and family members you didn't know, things that up until now might have been left undiscussed, and by discussing these things you might end up feeling closer to them, and develop stronger, more meaningful relationships.

And while we're on the topic of resources, here's my Linktree page, where you can find links to the entire Stark online universe, including my professional website, other books I've written, and various social media profiles. Please peruse, and feel free to reach out with any questions, comments, opinions, suggestions, or recipes.

linktr.ee/philstark

www.ingramcontent.com/pod-product-compliance
Ingram Content Group UK Ltd.
Pitfield, Milton Keynes, MK11 3LW, UK
UKHW022002190726
13853UKWH00004B/1691